Connect
SECOND EDITION

Jack C. Richards
Carlos Barbisan
with Chuck Sandy

Student's Book 1

CAMBRIDGE UNIVERSITY PRESS

Table of Contents

Syllabus iv

Unit 1 Back to School
Lesson 1 Classmates 2
Lesson 2 Hello. 4
Mini-review 6
Lesson 3 After school 8
Lesson 4 Names 10
Get Connected 12
Review 14

Unit 2 Favorite People
Lesson 5 Teachers and friends 16
Lesson 6 Favorite stars 18
Mini-review 20
Lesson 7 Birthdays 22
Lesson 8 E-pals 24
Get Connected 26
Review 28

Unit 3 Everyday Things
Lesson 9 What a mess! 30
Lesson 10 Cool things 32
Mini-review 34
Lesson 11 Favorite things 36
Lesson 12 Where is it? 38
Get Connected 40
Review 42

Unit 4 Around Town
Lesson 13 At the movies 44
Lesson 14 Downtown 46
Mini-review 48
Lesson 15 At the mall 50
Lesson 16 Any suggestions? 52
Get Connected 54
Review 56

Unit 5 Family and Home
Lesson 17 My family 58
Lesson 18 Family reunion 60
Mini-review 62
Lesson 19 My new city 64
Lesson 20 At home 66
Get Connected 68
Review 70

Unit 6 At School
Lesson 21 The media center 72
Lesson 22 Around school 74
Mini-review 76
Lesson 23 School subjects 78
Lesson 24 Spring Day 80
Get Connected 82
Review 84

Unit 7 Around the World
Lesson 25 People and countries 86
Lesson 26 Nationalities 88
Mini-review 90
Lesson 27 Holidays 92
Lesson 28 Important days 94
Get Connected 96
Review 98

Unit 8 Teen Time
Lesson 29 Favorite places 100
Lesson 30 Talent show 102
Mini-review 104
Lesson 31 School fashion 106
Lesson 32 Teen tastes 108
Get Connected 110
Review 112

Games 114

Get Connected Vocabulary Practice 122

Theme Projects 126

Word List 134

Syllabus

Connect Student's Book 1

Unit 1 Back to School

Lesson	Function	Grammar	Vocabulary
Lesson 1 Classmates	Introducing yourself	*What's your name?*	Ways to say hello
Lesson 2 Hello.	Greeting someone	*How are you?*	Greetings
Lesson 3 After school	Introducing others	*this is* (name)	Ways to say good-bye
Lesson 4 Names	Spelling names	Names	Common American names
Get Connected	Reading • Listening • Writing		
Theme Project	Make a personal information poster.		

Unit 2 Favorite People

Lesson	Function	Grammar	Vocabulary
Lesson 5 Teachers and friends	Talking about teachers and friends	*his / her* *Who's this?*	Teachers and classmates
Lesson 6 Favorite stars	Talking about favorite stars	*He's / She's . . .*	Stars and their jobs
Lesson 7 Birthdays	Talking about age	*How old . . . ?* *He's not / She's not*	Numbers 0–20
Lesson 8 E-pals	Talking about where someone is from	*Where . . . from?* *You're / I'm not*	Countries
Get Connected	Reading • Listening • Writing		
Theme Project	Make a poster about two people who work at your school.		

Unit 3 Everyday Things

Lesson	Function	Grammar	Vocabulary
Lesson 9 What a mess!	Describing who owns specific things	*This is / That's* + possessive	Things students own
Lesson 10 Cool things	Talking about interesting things	*What's this / that?*	Interesting objects
Lesson 11 Favorite things	Talking about favorite things	*What are these / those?*	Things students collect
Lesson 12 Where is it?	Talking about where things are located	*Where's / Where are . . . ?* *It's not / They're not . . .*	Objects in a bedroom
Get Connected	Reading • Listening • Writing		
Theme Project	Make an advertisement for an electronics store.		

Unit 4 Around Town

Lesson	Function	Grammar	Vocabulary
Lesson 13 At the movies	Asking where someone is	*Are you . . . ?*	Places in town
Lesson 14 Downtown	Describing where something is	*Is it . . . ?*	More places in town Locations
Lesson 15 At the mall	Talking about where people are	*Is she / Are they . . . ?*	Places in the mall
Lesson 16 Any suggestions?	Making suggestions	Suggestions for others Suggestions for you + others	At the beach
Get Connected	Reading • Listening • Writing		
Theme Project	Make a guide for visitors to your city.		

Unit 5 Family and Home	Lesson	Function	Grammar	Vocabulary
	Lesson 17 My family	Talking about family members	have / has	Numbers 21–100 Family members
	Lesson 18 Family reunion	Describing what someone is like	What's . . . like?	Appearance and personality traits
	Lesson 19 My new city	Describing new neighborhoods and friends	We're / They're; Our / Their	Adjectives to describe places and people
	Lesson 20 At home	Describing a home	It has . . .	Areas of a house
	Get Connected	Reading • Listening • Writing		
	Theme Project	Make a group photo album.		

Unit 6 At School	Lesson	Function	Grammar	Vocabulary
	Lesson 21 The media center	Talking about what is in a room	There's / There are . . . There's no / There are no . . .	Things in a media center
	Lesson 22 Around school	Asking about school facilities	Is there a / Are there any . . . ?	School facilities
	Lesson 23 School subjects	Describing a class schedule	on / at	School subjects Saying the time
	Lesson 24 Spring Day	Talking about time and when events begin	What time . . . ?	Special events
	Get Connected	Reading • Listening • Writing		
	Theme Project	Make a poster of a dream school ("cool school").		

Unit 7 Around the World	Lesson	Function	Grammar	Vocabulary
	Lesson 25 People and countries	Talking about where people are from	is / isn't; are / aren't in short answers	Countries
	Lesson 26 Nationalities	Describing famous people	isn't / aren't in statements	Nationalities
	Lesson 27 Holidays	Talking about holidays	When is . . . ?	Months of the year Holidays
	Lesson 28 Important days	Describing favorite months	in / on	Dates and ordinal numbers
	Get Connected	Reading • Listening • Writing		
	Theme Project	Make an informational booklet about different countries.		

Unit 8 Teen Time	Lesson	Function	Grammar	Vocabulary
	Lesson 29 Favorite places	Talking about favorite places	What's it like?	Adjectives to describe places
	Lesson 30 Talent show	Describing talents	can / can't	Talents
	Lesson 31 School fashion	Talking about school uniforms	What color is / are . . . ?	Clothing Colors
	Lesson 32 Teen tastes	Talking about likes and dislikes	love / like / don't like	Music Food
	Get Connected	Reading • Listening • Writing		
	Theme Project	Make a pair of bookmarks of healthy foods and activities.		

UNIT 1 Back to School

Lesson 1

Classmates

1 Saying hello

A It is the first day of school at Kent International School. Listen and practice.

Hi. I'm Nicole.
Hello. I'm Yoshi.
Hello. My name is Sandra.
Hi. I'm Jenny.
Hi. My name is Paulo.
Hello. I'm Tyler.

B Listen again. Write the names.

1. *Paulo*
2. _____
3. _____
4. _____
5. _____
6. _____

2 Language focus

A Jenny and Paulo meet. Listen and practice.

Jenny Hi. I'm Jenny.
What's your name?
Paulo My name is Paulo.
Jenny Nice to meet you, Paulo.
Paulo Nice to meet you, too.

> **What's your name?**
> What's your name?
> My name is Paulo.
> I'm Jenny.
>
> What's = What is   I'm = I am

B Complete the conversations. Listen and check. Then practice.

1. **Jenny** What's __your__ (you / your) name?
   Sandra _____ (My / Your) name is Sandra.

2. **Yoshi** Hello. _____ (I'm / You) Yoshi.
   Paulo Nice to meet _____ (you / your), Yoshi.

3. **Nicole** I'm Nicole. _____ (Is / What's) your name?
   Tyler _____ (My / You) name is Tyler.

4. **Sandra** Hi. My _____ (nice / name) is Sandra.
   Yoshi _____ (My / I'm) Yoshi. Nice to meet you.

3 Speaking

Introduce yourself to three classmates.

You Hello. I'm .... What's your name?
Classmate My name is ....
You Nice to meet you, ...
Classmate Nice to meet you, too.

Back to School 3

Lesson 2 Hello.

1 Greetings

Samantha greets people. Listen and practice.

Titles		Single	Married
Females	Miss	✓	☐
	Mrs.	☐	✓
	Ms.	✓	✓
Males	Mr.	✓	✓

2 Listening

Which greetings do you hear? Listen and check (✓) two greetings for each conversation.

	Good morning.	Good afternoon.	Good evening.	Hi.	Hello.
Conversation 1	☐	✓	☐	☐	✓
Conversation 2	☐	☐	☐	☐	☐
Conversation 3	☐	☐	☐	☐	☐
Conversation 4	☐	☐	☐	☐	☐

3 Language focus

A Ms. Davis and Sandra greet each other. Listen and practice.

Ms. Davis Good morning, Sandra. How are you today?
Sandra Fine, thank you. How about you?
Ms. Davis Great, thanks. Are you ready for the new school year?
Sandra Yes, I am.

B Study the language chart.

C Complete the conversations with the words in the boxes. Listen and check. Then practice.

☑ are ☐ not ☐ too ☐ you

1. **Tyler** Good morning. How ___are___ you?
   Sandra _____ bad, thanks. How about _____ ?
   Tyler Not _____ good.

☐ afternoon ☐ good ☐ how ☐ you

2. **Ms. Davis** Good _____ , Paulo. How are you today?
   Paulo OK. _____ about you?
   Ms. Davis _____ , thank _____ .

4 Speaking

Greet three classmates.

Good .... How are you?   .... How about you?

Back to School 5

Lessons 1 & 2 Mini-review

1 Language check

A Complete the chart with words in the box. Use two words twice.

☐ Miss ☐ Mrs. ☐ Mr. ☐ Ms.

	Single	Married
Females	Miss	_____
Males	_____	_____

B Number the sentences in the correct order.

1. ____ Nice to meet you, Tina.
   _1_ Hi. I'm Marco. What's your name?
   ____ My name is Tina.
   ____ Nice to meet you, too.

2. ____ Fine, thanks.
   ____ Yes, I am.
   ____ Good morning, Ms. Moss. How are you?
   ____ OK, thank you. How about you?
   ____ Are you ready for the new school year?

3. ____ Not bad.
   ____ OK, thanks. How are you?
   ____ Yes, I am.
   ____ Are you ready for class today?
   ____ Good afternoon, Mr. James. Sorry I'm late. How are you?

4. ____ Nice to meet you, Josh.
   ____ Are you ready for the new school year?
   ____ Hello. My name is Jim.
   ____ Yes, I am.
   ____ Hi, Jim. I'm Josh.
   ____ Nice to meet you, too.

C Complete the conversations with the sentences in the box.
Then practice.

☐ Hi, Wendy. ☐ Nice to meet you, Ethan. ☑ What's your name?
☐ How are you? ☐ Not bad.

First day of school

Wendy Hi. I'm Wendy. *What's your name?*
Ethan My name is Ethan.
Wendy _____

Second day of school

Ethan _____
Wendy Hello, Ethan. _____
Ethan Good, thanks. How about you?
Wendy _____

2 Listening

A What's next? Listen and check (✓) the correct response.

1. ☐ Great, thanks.
   ☑ I'm Joseph.

2. ☐ Thank you.
   ☐ Good morning.

3. ☐ Fine, thanks.
   ☐ My name is Jennifer.

4. ☐ Not too good.
   ☐ Nice to meet you.

5. ☐ Hello, Dan. Sorry I'm late.
   ☐ How about you?

6. ☐ Good evening, Elizabeth.
   ☐ Nice to meet you, too.

B Now listen to the complete conversations. Check your answers.

Go to page 114 for the Game.

Back to School 7

Lesson 3: After school

1 Language focus

A Nicole joins the basketball team. Listen and practice.

> **this is** (name)
> Mr. Diaz, **this is** Nicole Martel.
> Nicole, **this is** Mr. Diaz.

Tyler Hi, Nicole. How are you?
Nicole Good, thanks.

Tyler Mr. Diaz, this is Nicole Martel.

Tyler Nicole, this is Mr. Diaz.
Nicole Hi, Mr. Diaz. Nice to meet you.
Mr. Diaz Nice to meet you, too.

Mr. Diaz OK. Are you ready? Let's go!

B Introduce two classmates to each other.

> You ......, this is ....
> ......, this is ....
> **Classmate 1** Hi, ...
> **Classmate 2** Hi, ... Nice to meet you.

C Complete the conversations with the words in the box. Which conversation is an introduction? Circle it.

☐ are ☐ good ☐ hello ☑ is ☐ you

1. **Jenny** Hi, Mr. Diaz. This ___is___ Paulo Santos.
    Mr. Diaz Hello, Paulo.
    Paulo Nice to meet _____, Mr. Diaz.

2. **Tyler** _____, Sandra.
    Sandra Hi, Tyler. How _____ you?
    Tyler _____, thanks.

2 Listening

Are these conversations introductions? Listen and check (✓) Yes or No.

	Yes	No		Yes	No
Conversation 1	✓	☐	Conversation 4	☐	☐
Conversation 2	☐	☐	Conversation 5	☐	☐
Conversation 3	☐	☐			

3 Saying good-bye

A Listen and practice.

Good night, Mr. Diaz.
Good-bye, Paulo.
Bye, Tyler.
See you later.
See you tomorrow.
Bye-bye, Nicole.

B Complete the conversations. Then practice with a partner. Use your own information.

1. **A** Good-___bye___, Sue.   **B** _____ you later, Jack.
2. **A** _____ night, Mr. Lee.   **B** Bye-bye, Dave.
3. **A** Bye-bye, Kendra.   **B** See _____ tomorrow, Min!

Back to School 9

Lesson 4 — Names

1 Vocabulary

A Listen to these common American names. Then practice.

Girls' names			Boys' names		
Annie	Kaitlyn	Olivia	David	Matthew	Tyler
Elizabeth	Madison	Samantha	Ethan	Michael	William
Emma	Mia	Sophia	Jack	Ryan	Zachary
Hannah			John		

B Listen to the alphabet. Then practice.

Aa Bb Cc Dd Ee Ff Gg Hh Ii Jj Kk Ll Mm
Nn Oo Pp Qq Rr Ss Tt Uu Vv Ww Xx Yy Zz

C How do these students spell their names? Listen and write the names. Then practice.

1. Alex   2. _____   3. _____   4. _____   5. _____

2 Pronunciation — Syllables

A Study the pronunciation chart. Then listen and practice.

1 syllable	2 syllables	3 syllables
John	An nie	Za cha ry

B Listen to these names. How many syllables do they have?

1. Samantha 3   2. Jack ____   3. Ethan ____   4. Madison ____   5. David ____

3 Language focus

A Adriana gets a library card. Listen and practice.

Mr. Moore What's your name?
Adriana Adriana Moraes.
Mr. Moore Is that A-D-R-I-A-N-A?
Adriana Yes, that's right.
Mr. Moore And how do you spell your last name?
Adriana M-O-R-A-E-S.
Mr. Moore OK. Here's your card.

Names

First names	Last names
Yoshi	Sato
Jenny	Wilson
Tyler	Foster

How do you spell your last name?
M-O-R-A-E-S.

B Complete the conversation with your own information. Then practice with a classmate.

A What's your name?
B _____

A How do you spell your last name?
B _____

4 Speaking

Learn to spell your classmates' last names.

You Hi! What's your last name?
Classmate . . . .
You How do you spell your last name?
Classmate . . . .

Back to School 11

Get Connected
UNIT 1

Read

A Read the article quickly. Write the last names of the three people in the article.

1. _____   3. _____
2. _____

Meet Jayden, Amira, and Daniel!

Hi, friends! My name is Jayden. My last name is Hampton. **I like candy bars**, and I like basketball. Oh, and my nickname is Jay. What's your nickname?

Good afternoon! I'm Amira Moore. My nickname is Amy. My **dog's** name is Star. I like **sushi**! Nice to meet you. See you later.

Hello. I'm Daniel Reyes. My nickname is Dan. I like **music**, and I like school. I'm great today. How about you? How are you today?

Go to page 122 for the Vocabulary Practice.

B Read the article slowly. Check your answers in Part A.

C Circle the correct words to complete the sentences.

1. Jayden's last name is (Moore / (Hampton) / Reyes).
2. Jayden likes (basketball / school / sushi).
3. Amira's dog's name is (Reyes / Star / Moore).
4. Amira likes (sushi / candy bars / music).
5. Daniel's nickname is (Amy / Dan / Jay).
6. Daniel's (name / nickname / last name) is Reyes.

12   Unit 1

What's your name?

A Kevin and Megan introduce themselves. Listen and write *True* or *False*. Then correct the false statements.

1. Megan is a new student. _True._ _____
2. Kevin's last name is Bartelsman. _____ _____
3. Megan's first name is Jones. _____ _____
4. Megan's nickname is Peg. _____ _____
5. Kevin's nickname is Kev. _____ _____

B What do you think? Write *I agree* or *I disagree* (don't agree).

1. Nicknames are cool. _____
2. I like my name. _____
3. My name is easy to spell. _____
4. My friend's name is easy to spell. _____

Your turn

A Complete the chart.

First name	
Last name	
Nickname	
School	
How are you today?	
I like . . .	

B Write about yourself to your new e-pal. Use the chart in Part A to help you.

Hello! My name is _____   My last name is _____
_____
_____
_____

Back to School

Unit 1 Review

Language chart review

Personal information	Introductions

What's your name?
    My name is Emma.
    I'm Emma.
How do you spell your name?
    E-M-M-A.
How are you today?
    Great!
    Fine, thank you.
    Not too good.
	Hi. **I'm** Emma.
	Andrew, **this is** Meg.
	Meg, **this is** Andrew.

What's = What is
I'm = I am

A Complete the conversations with the sentences in the box.

- ☑ Hello, Mr. McDonald. How are you?
- ☐ Nice to meet you, too.
- ☐ Steven, this is Monica.
- ☐ Not bad, thank you.

1. **A** *Hello, Mr. McDonald. How are you?*
   B Good, thanks. How about you, Caroline?
   A _____

2. **A** _____
   B Hi, Monica. Nice to meet you.
   C _____

B Match the conversations from Part A to the pictures. Write the numbers.

C Meet Leigh and Lee. Complete the conversations.

❶ Hello. _What's_ your name?

My name _____ Leigh Jones.

Hi. _____ Lee, too.

❷ How do you spell _____ name?

L-E-E. _____ about you?

L-E-I-G-H.

❸ Hi, Mr. Garcia. _____ are you today?

Great, thanks.

_____ is my new friend, Leigh.

❹ Hi, Leigh. _____ to meet you.

Nice to meet _____, too, Mr. Garcia.

D Circle the word in each box that is different. Then complete the message with the colored letter from that word.

(H**e**llo.)	Good morn**i**ng.	N**o**t bad.	D**a**vid
Good n**i**ght.	G**o**od-bye.	Gr**e**at.	J**o**hn
B**y**e.	Good **a**fternoon.	Th**a**nk you.	Anni**e**
Go**o**d-bye.	Good **e**vening.	F**i**ne.	W**i**lliam

S e e y u l t r !

Go to page 126 for the Theme Project.

Back to School 15

Lesson 5: Teachers and friends

UNIT 2 Favorite People

1 Vocabulary

A Listen to Tyler talk about his photo album. Number the pictures. Then listen again and practice.

This is my *classmate*, Jenny.

This is my *best friend*, Paulo.

This is my *math teacher*, Mr. Stern.

This is my *science teacher*, Ms. Davis.

1

This is my *basketball coach*, Mr. Diaz.

This is my *computer partner*, Sandra.

B Write about three people at your school.

Ms. Davis is my science teacher.   2. _____

1. _____   3. _____

2 Language focus

A Tyler and his dad look at photos. Listen and practice.

> **Tyler** Look, Dad, this is my new basketball coach.
> **Mr. Foster** What's his name?
> **Tyler** His name is Mr. Diaz.
> **Mr. Foster** Who's this?
> **Tyler** This is my computer partner. Her name is Sandra.
> **Mr. Foster** And who's this?
> **Tyler** Dad! This is Paulo – my best friend.

his / her
What's **his** name?
    His name is Mr. Diaz.
What's **her** name?
    Her name is Sandra.

Who's this?
Who's this?
    This is my computer partner.
    My computer partner.

Who's = Who is

B Complete the conversations. Listen and check. Then practice.

1. **Mr. Foster** _Who's_ (Who's / What's) this?
   Tyler My math teacher.
   Mr. Foster What's _____ (his / her) name?
   Tyler _____ (His / Her) name is Mr. Stern.

2. **Tyler** This is my classmate.
   Mr. Foster _____ (What's / Who's) her name?
   Tyler _____ (His / Her) name is Jenny.

3. **Mr. Foster** And _____ (who's / what's) this?
   Tyler My science teacher. _____ (His / Her) name is Ms. Davis.

3 Pronunciation   Contractions with question words

A Listen. Notice the contractions *Who's* and *What's*. Then listen again and practice.

| Who's this? | What's her name? | What's his name? |

B Now practice the conversations in Exercise 2B.

Favorite People   17

Lesson 6: Favorite stars

1 Vocabulary

Look at the photos on Julia's Web site. Label the pictures with the words in the box. Then listen and practice.

- [ ] actor
- [✓] model
- [ ] soccer player
- [ ] TV star
- [ ] cartoon character
- [ ] singer
- [ ] tennis player

1. Gisele Bündchen — *model*
2. Eugenie Bouchard
3. Amazing Spider-Man
4. Neymar
5. Alicia Keys
6. Brad Pitt
7. Ryan Seacrest

2 Language focus

A Wendy, Julia, and Clare talk about their favorite stars. Listen and practice.

Wendy Who's this?
Julia Gisele Bündchen. She's my favorite model.
Clare And who's this?
Julia Neymar. He's my favorite soccer player.
Wendy So, who's your favorite actor?
Julia Brad Pitt. He's right here.
Clare Oh, I'm a Brad Pitt fan, too. I think he's cute.

He's / She's...
He's my favorite soccer player.
She's my favorite model.
He's = He is   She's = She is

B Write about these stars from Julia's Web site. Then listen and check.

1. (Gisele Bündchen) *This is Gisele Bündchen. She's a model.*
2. (Amazing Spider-Man) _____
3. (Eugenie Bouchard) _____
4. (Ryan Seacrest) _____
5. (Neymar) _____

3 Listening

Listen to students talk about their favorite stars. Check (✓) the correct stars.

1. ☑ actor   2. ☐ model   3. ☐ soccer player   4. ☐ cartoon character
   ☐ TV star   ☐ singer   ☐ tennis player   ☐ TV star

4 Speaking

Complete the chart with your favorite stars.
Then ask two classmates about their favorite stars.

	You	Classmate 1	Classmate 2
Actor			
Singer			
Cartoon character			

Who's your favorite ......?   My favorite ...... is ......

Favorite People 19

Lessons 5 & 6 Mini-review

1 Language check

A Dina introduces Olivia to Ryan. Complete the conversation. Then practice.

Dina Hi, Ryan. How ___are___ (is / are) you?
Ryan Great, thanks.
Dina Ryan, _____ (this / she) is Olivia. _____ (He's / She's) my science partner.
Ryan Nice to meet _____ (you / she), Olivia.
Olivia Nice to meet you, too. _____ (What's / Who's) your science partner, Ryan?
Ryan Rebecca.
Olivia _____ (What's / Who's) her last name?
Ryan Johnson.
Olivia Really? She's _____ (my / your) best friend!

Olivia   Dina   Ryan

B Complete the sentences with *He's*, *She's*, *His*, or *Her*.

1. This is Luiz. ___He's___ my partner in English class. _____ favorite class is science.

2. This is Lin. _____ my best friend. _____ favorite singer is Beyoncé.

3. Mr. Adams is my favorite teacher. _____ great. _____ first name is Ethan.

20 Unit 2

C Circle the correct words to complete the e-mail.

TO: raul.gm@cct.net
FROM: linda.nl@cct.net
SUBJECT: Hello!

Hi, Raul!

How are you? I'm fine.

This is (**my** / you) best friend. (Her / She) name is Mia.

(He's / She's) really nice. (What's / Who's) your best friend?

(What's / Who's) his or her name?

Mia's favorite actor is Chris Hemsworth. I think
(he's / his) a good actor. (He's / His) best movie is
Thor: The Dark World. (What's / Who's) your favorite star?

Your friend,
Linda

2 Listening

A Who is each person talking about? Listen and check (✓) the correct answers.

	An actor	A tennis player	A teacher	A best friend	A singer	A cartoon character
1.					✓	
2.						
3.						
4.						
5.						
6.						

B Now listen to the complete information. Check your answers.

Go to page 115 for the Game.

Lesson 7 — Birthdays

1 Numbers 0–20

A Listen to the numbers. Then practice.

0 zero (oh)	**5** five	**10** ten	**15** fifteen	**18** eighteen
1 one	**6** six	**11** eleven	**16** sixteen	**19** nineteen
2 two	**7** seven	**12** twelve	**17** seventeen	**20** twenty
3 three	**8** eight	**13** thirteen		
4 four	**9** nine	**14** fourteen		

B Listen and write the ages.

Name: Zach Shaw   Age: 17
Name: Leo Garcia   Age: _____
Name: Hannah Kirby Age: _____
Name: Lizzy Smith Age: _____
Name: Carla Mendez Age: _____
Name: Dan Ito   Age: _____

C Look at Part B. Write words for the ages.

1. Zach is _____seventeen_____ .
2. Hannah is _____ .
3. Lizzy is _____ .
4. Carla and Dan are _____ .
5. Leo is _____ .

2 Language focus

A Joy is at Dan's birthday party. Listen and practice.

Joy Happy birthday, Dan! How old are you today? Thirteen?
Dan No, I'm twelve. How old are you? Thirteen?
Joy No, I'm not thirteen. I'm only eleven. But my birthday is tomorrow.
Dan Really? Happy birthday!

> **How old . . . ?**
> How old are you? How old is she?
> **I'm** twelve. **She's** three.
>
> **He's not / She's not**
> **He's not** thirteen. He's twelve.
> **She's not** four. She's only three.

B Look at Exercise 1B on page 22. Answer the questions. Then listen and check.

1. How old is Carla? Thirteen? *No, she's not thirteen. She's twelve.*
2. How old is Hannah? Twelve? _____
3. How old is Leo? Eleven? _____
4. How old is Lizzy? Six? _____
5. How old is Dan? Ten? _____
6. How old is Zach? Eighteen? _____

3 Listening

A How old are these people today? Write your guesses in the chart.

	Chris	Anna	Andy	Joshua

Your guess	eleven			
Correct age				

B Compare answers. Then listen and write the correct ages in the chart.

> How old is Chris? I think he's eleven.

> I think he's thirteen.

4 Speaking

Learn the ages of four of your classmates.

You How old are you, ...?
Classmate I'm .... How old are you?
You I'm ....

Favorite People   23

Lesson 8: E-pals

1 Vocabulary

A Jenny and Paulo look at pictures of students and their e-pals. Where are they from? Listen and complete the sentences. Then listen again and practice.

1. Paulo is from ___Brazil___ .   His e-pal is from ___Peru___ .
2. Jenny is from _____ .   Her e-pal is from _____ .
3. Nicole is from _____ .   Her e-pal is from _____ .
4. Tyler is from _____ .   His e-pal is from _____ .
5. Sandra is from _____ .   Her e-pal is from _____ .
6. Yoshi is from _____ .   His e-pal is from _____ .

B Now draw lines to match the students with their e-pals.

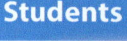
Students

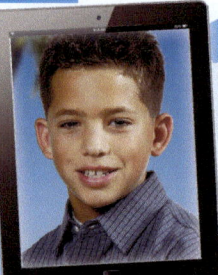
Paulo, Brazil (age 12)

Sandra, Mexico (age 12)

E-pals

Mike, Canada (age 12)

Miguel, Colombia (age 12)

2 Speaking

Talk about the people on the map.

You Mike is from Canada.
Classmate 1 How old is he?
Classmate 2 He's 12.

24 Unit 2

3 Language focus

A Paulo and Jenny talk about e-pals.
Listen and practice.

Paulo Hi, Jenny. Who's that?
Jenny That's Mike. He's my e-pal. He's 12.
Paulo Where's he from?
Jenny He's from Canada.
Paulo You're from Canada, too, right?
Jenny Canada? I'm not from Canada.
Paulo Really? Where are you from?
Jenny I'm from the U.S.
Paulo Oh, right. Sorry.

Where . . . from?

Where are you from?
  I'm from the U.S.
Where's he from?
  He's from Canada.

Where's = Where is

You're / I'm not

You're from Canada, right?
  I'm not from Canada.
  I'm from the U.S.

You're = You are

the U.S. = the United States

Jenny, the U.S.
(age 13)

Tyler, the U.S.
(age 12)

Nicole, Canada
(age 12)

Yoshi, Japan
(age 12)

Maria, Peru
(age 13)

Emma, Australia
(age 13)

Claudio, Venezuela
(age 14)

Lina, Portugal
(age 13)

B Complete the conversation. Listen and check. Then practice.

Paulo Here's a photo of my e-pal, Maria.
Jenny She's cute! _____ she from?
Paulo _____ from Peru.
Jenny Peru? You're from Peru, too, right?
Paulo Jenny, I'm _____ from Peru. I'm from Brazil.
Jenny I'm just kidding! I know that.

Favorite People 25

Get Connected
UNIT 2

Read

A Read the article quickly. Check (✓) the words you find.

☐ 1. model ☐ 3. singer ☐ 5. cartoon character
☐ 2. TV star ☐ 4. actor ☐ 6. a soccer player

SAM'S FAVORITES

Samantha Carter – "Sam"

Here's a photo of Shakira. She's my favorite singer. She's not from Mexico. She's from Colombia. Her nickname is Shaki. I think she's beautiful!

Here's my favorite TV star. His name is Kunal Nayyar, and he's from India. He's Raj on the **TV show** The Big Bang Theory. I like Kunal. He's great and so is The Big Bang Theory.

This is Bubbles, my favorite cartoon character. She's from Townsville – a fictional city in the U.S. She is one of The Powerpuff Girls. Bubbles is very **cute**!

Ellen Page is 21. She isn't from the U.S. She's from Canada. She's my favorite actor. She likes basketball and soccer. Her soccer nickname is "Peeps."

Meet my best friend, Tim. He's from Australia, not the U.S. He's 13. His favorite class is math and his favorite **sports** are tennis and basketball.

Go to page 122 for the Vocabulary Practice.

B Read the article slowly. Check your answers in Part A.

C Are these statements true or false? Write *True* or *False*. Then correct the false statements.

1. Shakira is from Mexico. <u>False.</u>   <u>She's from Colombia.</u>
2. Shakira's nickname is Shaki. _____
3. Kunal is a cartoon character. _____
4. Bubbles is very cute. _____
5. Ellen Page isn't from Canada. _____
6. Tim is Sam's favorite TV star. _____

She's so cute!

A 🎧 Andrew and Manny talk about Andrew's new science partner. Listen and circle the correct words.

1. Isabel is Andrew's new (classmate / (science partner) / best friend).
2. Isabel is from (Peru / Portugal / Brazil).
3. Isabel's nickname is (Cute / Manny / Izzy).
4. Andrew's favorite singer is (Jesse McCartney / Isabel / Justin Timberlake).
5. Andrew thinks (SpongeBob / Isabel / Spider-Man) is awesome.

B Are these statements true or false for you? Write *True* or *False*. Then correct the false statements. Use your own information.

1. Thirteen (13) is a good age. _____
2. Justin Timberlake is a great singer. _____
3. Cartoons are funny. _____
4. SpongeBob is a good cartoon character. _____

Your turn

A Complete the chart.

Who's your . . . ?	Name	Where's he / she from?	I think he / she is . . .
favorite classmate			
favorite teacher			
favorite coach			
favorite e-pal			

B Write about your favorite people. Use the chart in Part A to help you.

My best friend is _____. He's / She's from _____
_____. I think _____.
_____
_____

Favorite People 27

Unit 2 Review

Language chart review

The verb *be*			
Wh- questions	**Statements**	**I'm / He's / She's ...**	**My / His / Her ...**

How old are you?	**I'm** 16.
	   I'm not 18.
	You're 15.
	   You're not 14.
		I'm a singer.
		He's a model.
		She's a teacher.
			My name is Carla.
			His name is Steven.
			Her name is Ms. Kelly.

Where's he from?	**He's** from Brazil. **He's not** from Peru.	He's = He is She's = She is	
Where's she from?	**She's** from Canada. **She's not** from the U.S.		
Who's this?	**This is** my best friend.		
Where's = Where is Who's = Who is	You're = You are		

A Complete the sentences in the comic book with *I'm*, *he's*, *she's*, *my*, *his*, or *her*.

It's the year 2075. People can travel around the world in minutes. Kate meets her friends at the Global Café.

Kate and Her Global Friends

Hi. My name is Kate. I'm thirteen, and _____ from Australia.

This is _____ best Global friend. _____ name is Felicia. _____ from Mexico, and _____ fourteen.

This is Carlos. _____ from Peru. _____ my Global computer partner. _____ favorite class is computer science.

B Complete the questions with *Who, What, Where,* or *How.*
Then match each question to the correct answer.

1. _How_ old is Kate? _f_
2. _____ is she from? ____
3. _____ is her best friend? ____
4. _____ old is Felicia? ____
5. _____ is Carlos from? ____
6. _____ is the name of the café? ____

a. She's from Mexico.
b. Felicia.
c. He's from Peru.
d. She's fourteen.
e. Global Café.
f. She's thirteen.

C Read about these comic book characters. Then write about them.

Name: Seth Strong
Age: 15
Country: Canada

Name: Carla Cool
Age: 17
Country: Colombia

Name: Akio Adventure
Age: 12
Country: Japan

1. _His name is Seth._
   He's _____ .
   He's from _____ .

2. _____
   _____
   _____

3. _____
   _____
   _____

D Look again at Part C. Correct these sentences.

1. Seth is sixteen. _Seth is not sixteen. He's fifteen._
2. Seth is from the U.S. _____
3. Carla's last name is Strong. _____
4. Carla is from Venezuela. _____
5. Akio is from Portugal. _____
6. Akio is twenty. _____

Go to page 127 for the Theme Project.

Favorite People 29

Lesson 9: What a mess!

1 Vocabulary

A Matt and Tara are home from school. Look at the picture and write the names of the items. Use the words in the box. Then listen and practice.

☐ address book ☐ bag ☐ brush ☐ eraser ☐ notebook ☐ pencil case
☑ backpack ☐ book ☐ camera ☐ hat ☐ pen ☐ umbrella

1. backpack
2. _____
3. _____
4. _____
5. _____
6. _____
7. _____
8. _____
9. _____
10. _____
11. _____
12. _____

B Look at Part A. Listen to Tara and Matt. Are their statements true or false? Write T (true) or F (false).

1. Tara T   2. Matt ____   3. Tara ____   4. Matt ____   5. Tara ____

UNIT 3 Everyday Things

30

2 Language focus

A The living room is a mess. Listen and practice.

Mrs. Price Matt!
Matt Yes, Mom?
Mrs. Price Look at your things! What a mess!
Matt My things? This is Tara's pen, and that's her book.
Tara Yes, but that's Matt's hat, and . . .

This is / That's + possessive

This is Tara's pen.
That's Matt's hat.
That's = That is

B Complete the sentences with *This is* or *That's*. Then listen and check.

1

This is Matt's camera.
That's his pencil case.

2

_____ Matt's notebook.
_____ his umbrella.

3

_____ Tara's eraser.
_____ her book.

4

_____ Tara's address book.
_____ her brush.

3 Speaking

Talk about your classmates' things.

This is Roberto's pencil case.   That's Anna's . . . .

Everyday Things

Lesson 10 — Cool things

1 Vocabulary

A Complete the sentences with the words in the box. Then listen and practice.

- [ ] an alarm clock
- [ ] a cell phone
- [ ] an MP3 player
- [ ] a TV (television)
- [ ] a calculator
- [ ] a laptop
- [ ] a desktop computer
- [✓] a video game

1. This is _a video game_ . That's _____ .

2. This is _____ . That's _____ .

3. This is _____ . That's _____ .

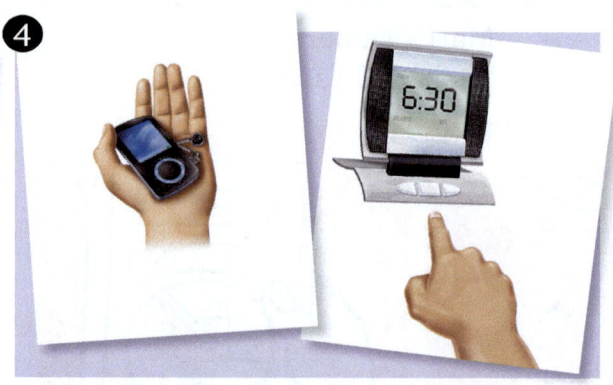

4. This is _____ . That's _____ .

B Write *a* or *an* before each word.

1. _an_ address book
2. ____ brush
3. ____ camera
4. ____ pencil case
5. ____ eraser
6. ____ hat
7. ____ umbrella
8. ____ backpack

> **a / an**
>
> **a** + consonant
>   a TV
>   a cell phone
>
> **an** + vowel sound
>   an alarm clock
>   an MP3 player

C Listen to the sounds. What do you hear? Who can answer first?

> That's an alarm clock.

2 Language focus

A Sandra and Jenny look at interesting things. Listen and practice.

> **What's this / that?**
> What's this? What's that?
> **It's** a calculator. **It's** a video game.
>
> It's = It is

Sandra Hey, Jenny. What's this?
         A cell phone?
Jenny   No, it's a calculator.
Sandra Hmm. It's weird.
         And what's that?
Jenny   It's a old video game.
Sandra Wow! It's cool.

B Complete the conversation with the words in the box. Listen and check. Then practice.

```
☐ a      ☐ cool    ☐ that's   ☐ what's
☐ an     ☐ it's    ☑ this
```

Liz   What's ___this___ ?
Ted   It's _____ new tablet.
Liz   Wow! It's _____ .
Ted   Yeah. _____ also _____ e-book reader.
Jill Really? And _____ that?
Ted   Oh, _____ a piano keyboard.
Jill Hmm . . . wireless piano keyboard?
Ted   Yes. It's a really cool tablet.

3 Listening

Listen to the conversations. Circle the correct things.

1. a TV / a laptop
2. a calculator / a cell phone
3. a cell phone / a video game
4. an alarm clock / an MP3 player

Everyday Things   33

Mini-review

1 Language check

A Check (✓) *a* or *an* for each sentence. Then match the sentences to the correct picture.

	a	an	Picture
1. This is ____ eraser.	☐	✓	d
2. It's ____ pen.	☐	☐	___
3. That's ____ TV.	☐	☐	___
4. It's ____ laptop.	☐	☐	___
5. This is ____ MP3 player.	☐	☐	___
6. That's ____ umbrella.	☐	☐	___

a

b

c

d

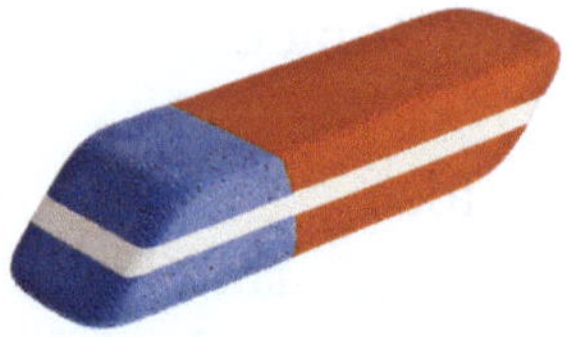

e

f

34   Unit 3

B These classmates are at the Museum of Technology. What do they say? Write sentences with *This is* or *That's*.

1. **Vera:** *That's a TV.*

2. **Jerry:** _____

3. **Lisa:** _____

4. **Miguel:** _____

2 Listening

Are these things Joe's or Suzanne's? Listen and write *J* (Joe) or *S* (Suzanne).

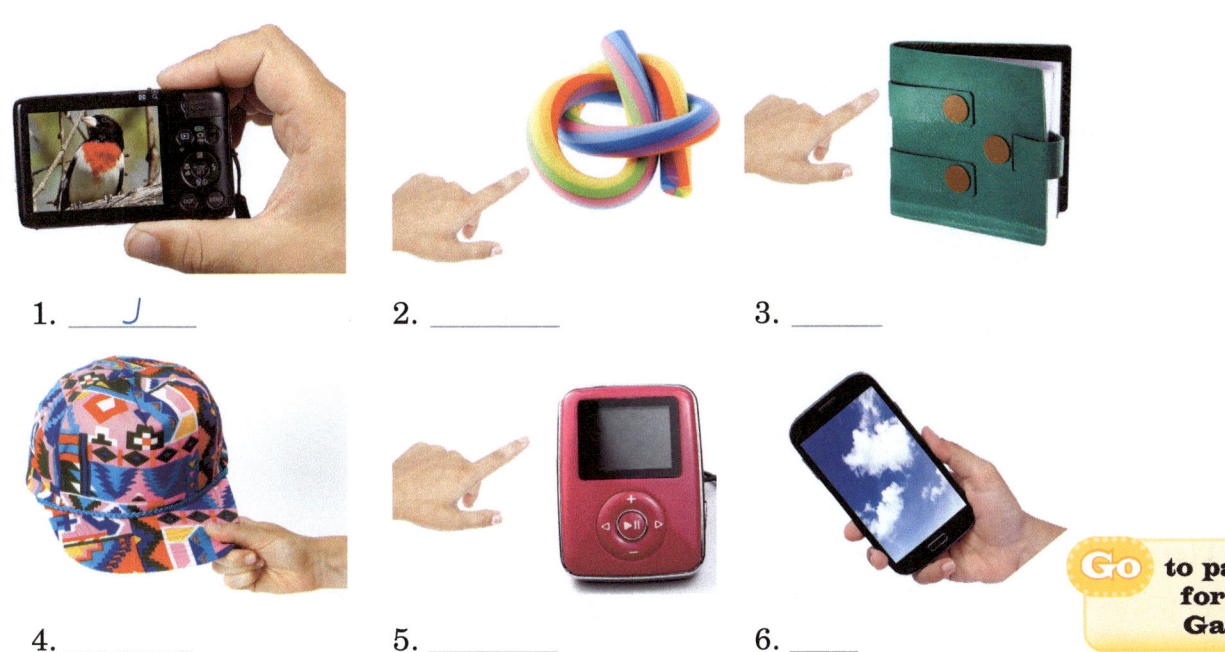

1. __J__   2. _____   3. _____

4. _____   5. _____   6. _____

Go to page 116 for the Game.

Lesson 11 — Favorite things

1 Vocabulary

A Label the photos of Nicole's and Yoshi's favorite things with the words in the box. Then listen and practice.

☑ bicycle ☐ comic books ☐ posters ☐ trading cards ☐ T-shirts ☐ watch

1. bicycle
2.
3.
4.
5.
6.

B What are your favorite things? Tell your classmates.

> My favorite things are my ......, my ......, and my ....

2 Pronunciation — Plural nouns

A Study the pronunciation chart. Then listen and practice.

No extra syllables	Extra syllable
book → books bag → bags	watch → watches case → cases

B Listen. Which plural nouns have extra syllables? Circle them.

1. hats
2. games
3. (coaches)
4. friends
5. brushes
6. boxes

36 Unit 3

3 Language focus

A There's a charity drive at school. Listen and practice. Then study the language chart.

Mr. Mori Hi, Paul. Tell me about your things. What are these?
Paul They're my favorite T-shirts. They're too small now.
Mr. Mori Oh, they're nice. And what are those?
Paul Those are my old watches.
Mr. Mori They're cool. Thanks, Paul.

What are these / those?	
What are these?	**What are those?**
These are T-shirts.	**Those are** watches.
They're T-shirts.	**They're** watches.

They're = They are

B Look at the picture. Complete the conversation with *these*, *those*, or *they're*. Listen and check. Then practice.

Ms. Garcia So, what are ___those___ , Monica?
Monica They're my comic books.
Ms. Garcia Hmm. _____ very interesting.
Monica _____ are my trading cards.
Ms. Garcia Oh, they're nice. What's in this box?
Monica _____ my old books.
Ms. Garcia Monica, _____ your English books!
Monica Yeah. They're from last year.

4 Speaking

Look at the things in the pictures on pages 36 and 37. Ask and answer questions.

What are these?   They're T-shirts.   What's this?   It's a / an ……… .

Everyday Things

Lesson 12: Where is it?

1 Vocabulary

A David is late for school. Where are his things?
Match the two parts of each sentence.
Then listen and practice.

1. David's books are _f_
2. His basketball is ____
3. His brush is ____
4. His watch is ____
5. His bag is ____
6. The photos are ____

a. under the bed.
b. in the wastebasket.
c. on the wall.
d. on the dresser.
e. next to the chair.
f. on the desk.

in

under

next to

on

B Look at David's room. Complete the sentences with
in, *under*, *next to*, or *on*.

1. David's alarm clock is __on__ the dresser.
2. His hat is _____ the bed.
3. His wastebasket is _____ the desk.
4. His posters are _____ the wall.
5. His books are _____ the camera.
6. His pencils are _____ the bag.

the
the desk
the books

38   Unit 3

2 Language focus

Complete the conversation. Listen and check. Then practice.

> **Where's / Where are . . . ?**
> **Where's** my bag?
> It's under the bed.
> **Where are** my pencils?
> They're in your bag.
>
> **It's not / They're not . . .**
> **It's not** on the desk.
> **They're not** in my pencil case.

David Dad! I'm late. Where are my pencils? They're not in my pencil case.
Mr. Evans They're in your bag.
David OK, but where's my bag? It's not on the desk.
Mr. Evans It's under the bed.
David Oh, right. Thanks. Oh! <u>Where are</u> my books? _____ in my bag!
Mr. Evans _____ next to your computer.
David And _____ my watch? _____ on the dresser.
Mr. Evans _____ in the wastebasket, David!

3 Listening

Where's the backpack? Listen and number the pictures.

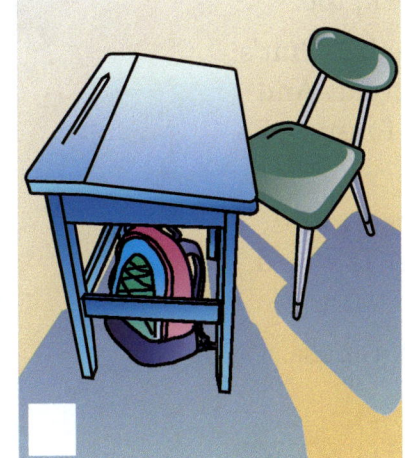

4 Speaking

Look at the picture on page 38. Make true and false statements. Your classmate says *Yes* or *No* and corrects the false statements.

You The bag is under the bed.
Classmate Yes.
You The books are next to the desk.
Classmate No. They're not next to the desk. They're on the desk.

Everyday Things

Get Connected
UNIT 3

Read

A Read the article quickly. Who's Maxie?

_____

A Really Cool Tree House

Meet Pete. He's a really interesting **teenager**. This is his **virtual tree house**. It's really cool.

Look next to the desk. What's that? It's Pete's pet **spider**. Her name is Angelina. She's a very nice spider.

Where's the wastebasket? It's under the desk. Where's the laptop? It's on the desk. And there's a photo on the desk, too.

And who's that next to the chair? That's Coco. She's Pete's **cat**. She's great. And that's Maxie, Pete's dog. He's funny – he **smiles**!

Look at the wall. There's a poster and a clock on the wall. The poster is weird. It's of Pete's favorite band.

Pete's virtual tree house isn't a mess. Is your room a mess?

Go to page 123 for the **Vocabulary Practice.**

B Read the article slowly. Check your answer in Part A.

C Answer the questions.

1. Where's the spider? _It's / She's next to the desk._
2. Where's the wastebasket? _____
3. Where are the laptop and the photo? _____
4. Where's Coco? _____
5. Where are the clock and the poster? _____

40   Unit 3

It's in your bag!

A 🔊 Tim and Katie talk about where Tim's MP3 player is. Listen and write *True* or *False*. Then correct the false statements.

1. Tim and Katie are late. _True._ _____
2. Tim's MP3 player is in his bag. _____
3. Tim's cell phone is a calculator, too. _____
4. His video game is on the dresser. _____
5. A spider is on the bed. _____

B What do you think? Write *I agree* or *I disagree* (don't agree).

1. I think cell phones are great. _____
2. I think video games are interesting. _____
3. I think MP3 players are cool. _____
4. I think spiders are weird. _____

Your turn

A Imagine a virtual classroom. Check (✓) the items in the classroom.

- ☐ bag   ☐ chair   ☐ computer   ☐ eraser   ☐ pen   ☐ TV
- ☐ books   ☐ clock   ☐ desk   ☐ notebook   ☐ poster ☐ wastebasket

B Write about your virtual classroom. Use the words in Part A to help you.

This is my virtual classroom. There's a wastebasket next ...

Everyday Things

Unit 3 Review

Language chart review

this / that / these / those questions and statements a / an	
This is a camera. What's this? It's a camera. That's an address book. What's that? It's an address book.	These are pens. What are these? They're pens. Those are comic books. What are those? They're comic books.
That's = That is It's = It is	They're = They are
Possessive 's	
This is Paul's backpack. These are Eva's pencils.	

A Ben and Lee are at camp. Look at the picture. Then complete the conversation.

Lee Hey, Ben. What are ____those____ (these / those) ?
Ben _____ (It's / They're) my favorite comic books.
Lee Oh, I see. _____ (Who's / What's) on the cover?
Ben _____ (He's / They're) my favorite superhero.
Lee And what's _____ (that / those) on the floor?
Ben It's _____ (a / an) sports magazine. I love soccer!
Lee And _____ (what's / who's) that?
Ben It's _____ (a / an) tablet.
Lee Wow! It's really nice. And what's _____ (this / that) in your backpack?
Ben _____ (It's / They're) my new camera.

B The names of seven more things are in the pencil. Circle them. Then write them in the chart. Use *a* or *an* for the singular words.

television watches cameras cellphone umbrellas tradingcards bicycle addressbook

Singular	Plural
a television	

Language chart review

Where's / Where are...?		Prepositions
Where's my cell phone?	**It's not** in my bag. It's on the desk.	in on
Where are my books?	**They're not** next to my computer. They're under the bed.	next to under

C Look at the picture. Then correct the sentences.

1. The books are on the desk. *They're not on the desk. They're on the bed.*
2. The pencils are next to the backpack. _____
3. The umbrella is next to the dresser. _____
4. The hat is on the bed. _____

D Look again at the picture in Part C. Write questions and answers about the other things.

1. Q: *Where's the basketball?* A: *It's next to the dresser.*
2. Q: _____ A: _____
3. Q: _____ A: _____
4. Q: _____ A: _____

Go to page 128 for the Theme Project.

Everyday Things

Lesson 13: At the movies

1 Vocabulary

A Where are Jenny and her friends? Listen and match the two parts of each sentence.

> *at*
> at the newsstand

1. Jenny is _e_ .
2. Tyler is ____ .
3. Sandra is ____ .
4. Nicole is ____ .
5. Yoshi is ____ .
6. Paulo is ____ .

a at the newsstand

b at the Internet café

c at the restaurant

d at the bus stop

e at the movie theater

f at the shoe store

B Listen again and check your answers in Part A. Then practice.

2 Listening

Look at the photos in Exercise 1. Where are the people? Listen and number the places.

____ Internet café   ____ newsstand   _1_ restaurant
____ movie theater   ____ shoe store   ____ bus stop

UNIT 4 Around Town

3 Language focus

Are you . . . ?
Are you still at home?
Are you near the movie theater?
Yes, I am.
No, I'm not.

A Jenny is at the movie theater. All of her friends are late! Listen and practice.

Tyler Hello?
Jenny Tyler, this is Jenny. It's really late. Are you still at home?
Tyler No, I'm not.
Jenny Oh. Are you near the movie theater?
Tyler Yes, I am. I'm at the bus stop.
Jenny Well, please hurry. You're late!
Tyler OK. I'm sorry.

B Complete the conversations. Listen and check. Then practice.

1. **Sandra** Hello?
   Jenny Hi, Sandra. Where are you? Are ___you___ near the movie theater?
   Sandra Yes, I _____ . I'm at the shoe store.
   Jenny _____ you with Paulo?
   Sandra No, I'm _____ .
   Jenny OK. Hurry. It's late!

2. **Paulo** Hello?
   Jenny Hi, Paulo. You're late! _____ _____ near the movie theater?
   Paulo No, _____ _____ . I'm still at home.
   Jenny Oh, no, Paulo! Hurry!
   Paulo I'm kidding. I'm at the newsstand.

4 Speaking

Complete these questions. Then interview a classmate.

Are you . . . ?	Yes	No
Are you _____ years old? (*age*)	☐	☐
Are you a _____ player? (*sport*)	☐	☐
Are you a _____ fan? (*favorite star*)	☐	☐
Are you from _____ ? (*city* or *town*)	☐	☐

Are you 12 years old?   Yes, I am.

Around Town   45

Lesson 14 Downtown

1 Vocabulary

A Look at the map. Complete the sentences. Then listen and practice.

1. The drugstore is _____on_____ Jefferson Street.
2. The department store is _____ the movie theater.
3. The parking lot is _____ the movie theater.
4. The bank is _____ the restaurant and the shoe store.
5. The subway station is _____ the shoe store.
6. The park is _____ the school.

on

in front of

behind

across from

between

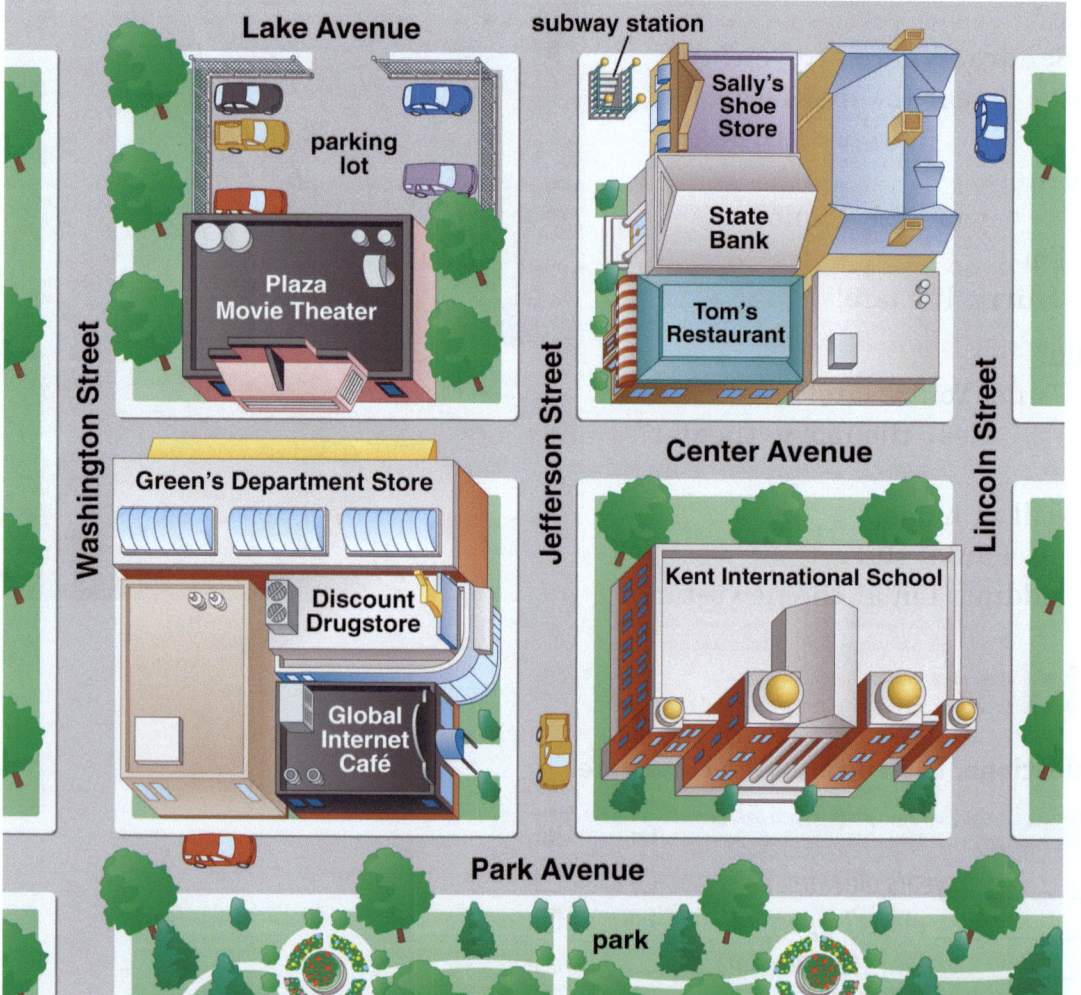

B Look at the places on the map. Make true and false statements. A classmate answers *True* or *False*.

— The parking lot is behind the movie theater.
— True.

46 Unit 4

2 Language focus

A Jackie and Lizzy are downtown. Listen and practice.

> **Is it...?**
> Is it across from the Internet café?
> Yes, it is.
> No, it's not.

Jackie I'm hungry! Let's go to Tom's Restaurant.
Lizzy   OK. Where is it?
Jackie I think it's on Park Avenue.
Lizzy   Oh. Is it across from the Internet café?
Jackie No, it's not. It's next to the bank.
Lizzy   But the bank is on Jefferson Street.
Jackie Uh-oh. I'm lost! Let's look at the map!

B Write questions about the map on page 46. Then practice with a classmate.

1. *Is the parking lot behind the shoe store?*
2. _____
3. _____
4. _____
5. _____

> Is the parking lot behind the shoe store?

> No, it's not. It's behind the movie theater.

3 Pronunciation *Yes / No* questions

Listen. Notice the intonation in the questions. Then listen again and practice.

A Is the school on Park Avenue?
B Yes, it is.

A Is the restaurant in front of the drugstore?
B No, it's not.

4 Speaking

Think of a place in your town or city. Your classmates guess the place. Use the correct intonation.

Classmate 1 Is it near the school?
You   Yes, it is.
Classmate 2 Is it on Miller Avenue?
You   No, it's not.
Classmate 3 Is it across from the school?
You   Yes, it is.
Classmate 4 Is it the park?
You   Yes, it is.

Around Town 47

Lessons 13 & 14 Mini-review

1 Language check

A Carlos and Anna are at a soccer game. Complete the conversations with *I am, I'm not, it is,* or *it's not.* Then practice.

Carlos Hi. Are you Anna Jones?
Anna Yes, _I am_ .
Carlos I'm in your science class.
Anna Oh, right . . . GO, TIGERS, GO!
Carlos Are you from Canada, Anna?
Anna Uh, no, _____ .
I'm from the U.S.
Carlos Are you on a soccer team?
Anna No, _____ . I'm just a fan. GO! GO!
(Ring! Ring!)
Carlos Anna, is that your cell phone?
Anna Oh! Yes, _____ . Thanks.

Anna Hello?
Mrs. Jones Anna, are you still at school?
Anna Uh, no, _____ .
A GOAL! YAY, TIGERS!
Mrs. Jones Anna, are you at the soccer field?
Anna Well, yes, _____ .
Is that OK?
Mrs. Jones No, _____ !
It's very late.
Anna But, Mom, . . .

B Complete these questions. Then practice with a classmate.

1. _Are_ you a soccer fan?
2. _____ you 12 years old?
3. _____ your English class interesting?
4. _____ you a good student?
5. _____ your school nice?
6. _____ your home near the school?

Are you a soccer fan?   No, I'm not.

C Look at the map. Then correct the mistakes in the e-mail.

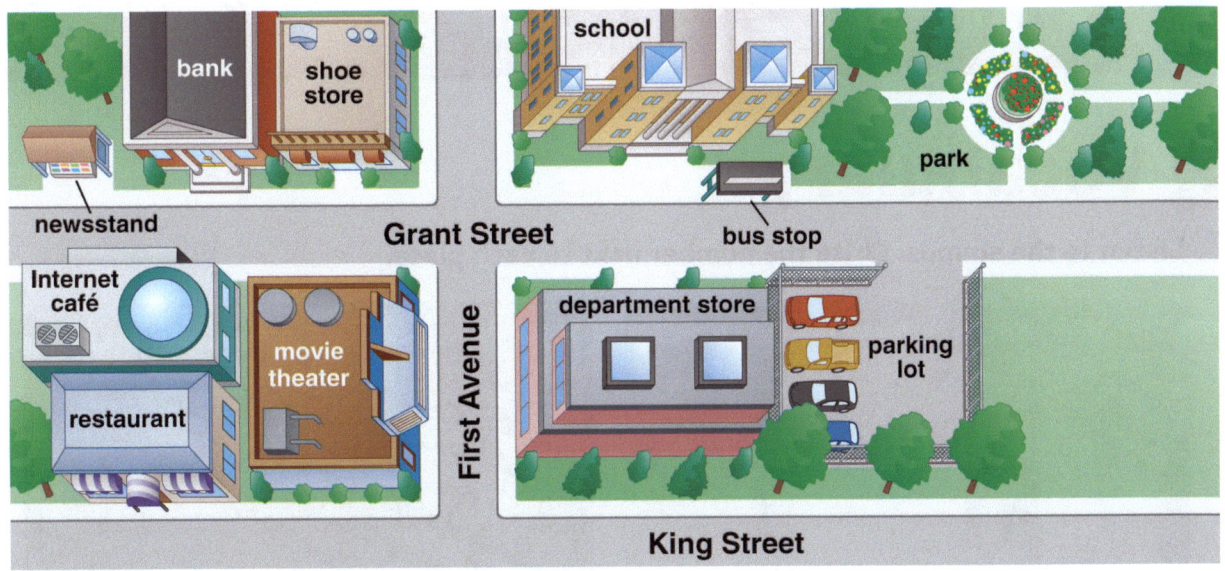

TO: donna.bee@cct.net
FROM: carlos.ft@cct.net
SUBJECT: Hi!

Hi, Donna!

How are you? I'm ~~on~~ *at* the Internet café. <u>Is</u> you still at home? Meet me <u>on</u> the department store in 15 minutes. It's <u>next to</u> the school, and it's <u>in front of</u> the parking lot.

See you soon,
Carlos

2 Listening

Look at the map in Exercise 1C. Listen and answer the questions. Write *No, it's not,* or *Yes, it is.*

1. *No, it's not.*
2. _____
3. _____
4. _____
5. _____
6. _____

Go to page 117 for the Game.

Around Town 49

Lesson 15: At the mall

1 Vocabulary

A Listen to the sounds. Write the number next to each place.

☐ skating rink

☐ music store

`1` bowling alley

☐ candy store

☐ bookstore

☐ video arcade

B Listen and check. Then practice.

C Write about three of your favorite places.

<u>My favorite music store is Virgo Beat Music.</u>

1. _____
2. _____
3. _____

50 Unit 4

2 Language focus

A Yoshi and Paulo are at the mall with their friends. Listen and practice.

Yoshi Where is everybody?
Paulo Well, Tyler and Jenny are at the video arcade.
Yoshi What about Nicole? Is she there, too?
Paulo No, she's not. She's with Sandra.
Yoshi Oh. Are they at the skating rink?
Paulo No, they're not . . . They're at the movie theater.
Yoshi Oh, no! Let's hurry!

> **Is she / Are they . . . ?**
> **Is she** at the video arcade?
>   Yes, she is.
>   No, she's not.
> **Are they** at the skating rink?
>   Yes, they are.
>   No, they're not.

B Read the conversation again. Complete the questions and then answer them. Then listen and check.

1. (Yoshi) <u>Is he</u> with Nicole?
   <u>No, he's not.</u>
2. (Jenny) _____ at the video arcade? _____
3. (Yoshi and Paulo) _____ at the mall? _____
4. (Tyler) _____ with Yoshi? _____
5. (Nicole) _____ with Tyler and Jenny? _____
6. (Nicole and Sandra) _____ at the skating rink? _____

3 Listening

A It's two hours later. Where are Paulo and his friends now? Listen and check (✓) the correct places.

	Candy store	Music store	Bookstore	Video arcade
Paulo	☐	☐	☐	☐
Jenny	☐	☐	☐	☐
Tyler	☐	☐	☐	☐
Nicole	☐	☐	☐	☐

B Compare answers with a classmate.

> Is Paulo at the music store?

> No, he's not. He's at the . . . .

Around Town 51

Lesson 16 — Any suggestions?

1 Vocabulary

A Look at the people at the beach. Listen to the suggestions and practice.

B Now write a suggestion for each person below. Use Part A to help you.

I'm **tired**.   I'm **thirsty**.   I'm **hungry**.   I'm **hot**.   I'm **bored**.
Sit down.

2 Listening

What's the problem with these people? Listen and check (✓) the correct problem.

1. ☐ She's hot.   2. ☐ He's bored.   3. ☐ They're thirsty.   4. ☐ She's tired.
   ☐ She's tired.   ☐ He's hungry.   ☐ They're hungry.   ☐ She's bored.

52 Unit 4

3 Language focus

Suggestions for others
Have a soda.
Suggestions for you + others
Let's go together.

A Matt and Chris are at the beach. Listen and practice.

Matt I'm thirsty.
Chris So go to a café, and have a soda.
Matt Good idea, but, um . . .
Chris What's wrong?
Matt Well, my money is at home.
Chris That's OK. I have money for two sodas. Let's go together.
Matt Great! Thanks, Chris!

B Complete the conversations with *go, have, sit,* or *play*. Listen and check. Then practice.

1. **A** Let's __play__ basketball.
   B But it's really hot.
   A Yeah – you're right. Let's _____ to the beach.
   B Good idea. Let's _____ swimming.

2. **A** I'm tired.
   B So _____ down.
   A OK. But I'm thirsty, too.
   B Then _____ to a café, and _____ a soda.

3. **A** Let's _____ a sandwich. I'm hungry.
   B Well, I'm not really hungry, but I am thirsty!
   A Oh. So _____ a soda.
   B OK. Let's _____ to a café.

4. **A** I'm really bored.
   B Me, too. Let's _____ to a video arcade.
   A But my money is at home.
   B Then let's _____ tennis in the park.
   A OK.

4 Speaking

Make suggestions. Use your own information or ideas.

I'm . . . .   So . . . .   I'm . . . .   Me, too. Let's . . . .

Around Town 53

Get Connected
UNIT 4

Read

A Read the Web site information quickly. Write the names of three places at West Edmonton Mall.

1. _____ 3. _____
2. _____

West Edmonton Mall

Welcome to the **biggest** mall in North America! We have interesting things for everybody.

Are you bored? Play **paintball** at Mad Existence Paintball. It's messy and it's weird, but it's very cool.

Are you hot? Go to the World Waterpark and play on the **waterslides**. It's across from the movie theaters.

Are you hungry and thirsty? Go to Jungle Jim's restaurant. It's on Bourbon Street. Sit down in the **jungle** and have a sandwich and a soda.

Look around the stores here, too! Are you a soccer fan? Go to Soccer Freak for your favorite soccer things. It's behind Sears department store. Or go to Comic King and look at comic books for your comic book collection. They have everybody's favorite comic books.

So hurry to Edmonton Mall – we have an **amusement park**, too!

Go to page 123 for the **Vocabulary Practice**.

B Read the article slowly. Check your answers in Part A.

C Answer the questions.

1. Is the West Edmonton Mall in South America? _No, it's not._
2. Is paintball a game? _____
3. Are the movie theaters across from the World Waterpark? _____
4. Is Jungle Jim's a soccer store? _____
5. Is Soccer Freak in front of the department stores? _____
6. Are the comic books in Soccer Freak? _____

54 Unit 4

I'm so bored!

A 🎧 **Judy and Anna talk about going to the mall. Listen and answer the questions.**

1. Are Anna and Judy at the mall? _No, they're not._
2. Is George's restaurant behind the video arcade? _____
3. Is Paul at the video arcade? _____
4. Is the music store between the video arcade and the bookstore? _____
5. Where's the bank? _____

B **What do you think? Write *I agree* or *I disagree* (don't agree).**

1. I think malls are fun. _____
2. I think video arcades are cool. _____
3. I think bookstores are interesting. _____
4. I think music stores are great. _____

Your turn

A **What are your four favorite places in your neighborhood or mall? Where are they? Complete the chart.**

Place	Where is it?
Example: Nick's Video Arcade	across from the school
1.	
2.	
3.	
4.	

B **Write sentences about three or four of the places in your neighborhood or mall. Use the chart in Part A to help you.**

In my neighborhood, my favorite _____ is _____
_____ . It's _____ . It's really cool.

Around Town

Unit 4 Review

Language chart review

Yes / No questions and short answers with be			Prepositions
Are you near the restaurant?	Yes, **I am**.	No, **I'm not**.	on
Is Yoshi at the video arcade?	Yes, **he is**.	No, **he's not**.	in front of
Is Sandra with Tyler?	Yes, **she is**.	No, **she's not**.	across from
Is the café near the movie theater?	Yes, **it is**.	No, **it's not**.	behind
Are Jenny and Paulo at the café?	Yes, **they are**.	No, **they're not**.	between

A Write questions with the correct forms of *be*. Then look at the picture, and answer the questions.

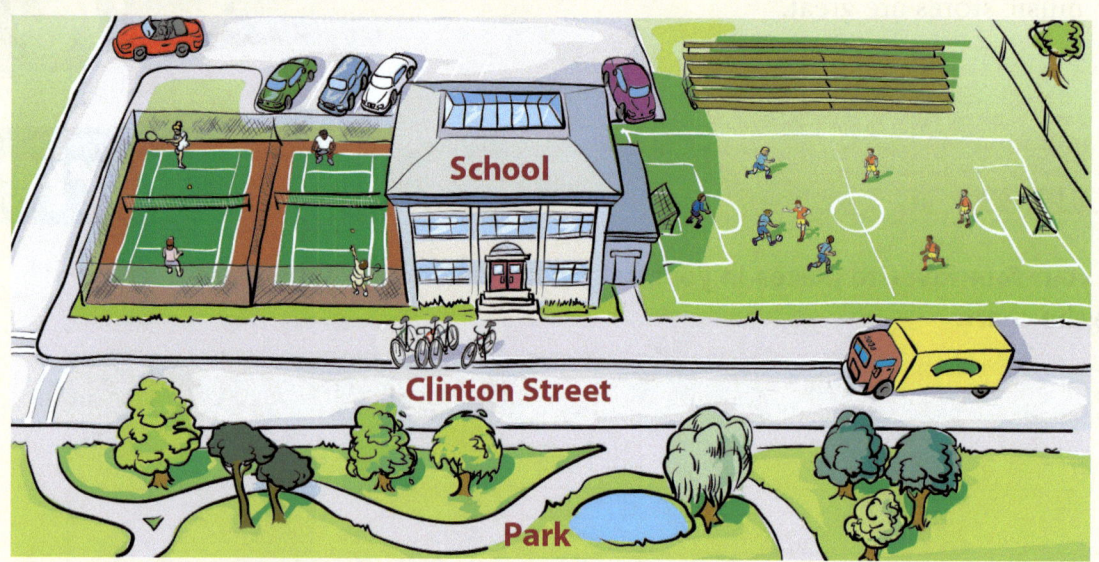

1. the school / behind the park

    Q: *Is the school behind the park?* **A:** *No, it's not.*

2. the bicycles / behind the school

    Q: _____ **A:** _____

3. the soccer field / across from the park

    Q: _____ **A:** _____

4. the parking lot / in front of the school

    Q: _____ **A:** _____

5. the school / between the tennis courts and the soccer field

    Q: _____ **A:** _____

6. the school / on Clinton Street

    Q: _____ **A:** _____

B Look at the pictures. Complete the questions and answers.

1. Q: _Are they_ at the restaurant?
   A: _Yes, they are._

2. Q: _____ at the movie theater?
   A: _____

3. Q: _____ at the newsstand?
   A: _____

4. Q: _____ at the café?
   A: _____

5. Q: _____ at the bus stop?
   A: _____

Language chart review

Suggestions for others	Suggestions for you + others
Play volleyball.	**Let's go** swimming.
Sit down.	**Let's have** a sandwich.
Have a soda.	**Let's sit** down.

C Write a suggestion for each situation. Use the expressions in the box or your own ideas.

☐ go   ☐ go swimming   ☑ have a soda   ☐ play a video game   ☐ sit down

1. You and your friends are thirsty. _Let's have a soda._
2. Your brother is tired. _____
3. You and your sister are late for a movie. _____
4. Your friend is hot. _____
5. You and your friends are bored. _____

Go to page 129 for the Theme Project.

Around Town 57

Lesson 17 — My family

1 Numbers 21–100

Listen to the numbers. Then practice.

21 twenty-one   22 twenty-two   23 twenty-three
24 twenty-four   25 twenty-five   26 twenty-six
27 twenty-seven 28 twenty-eight 29 twenty-nine

30 thirty 40 forty 50 fifty 60 sixty 70 seventy 80 eighty 90 ninety 100 one hundred

2 Vocabulary

A Meet Sonia's family. Listen and practice.

This is my sister, Jen. She's 21. This is my brother, Eddie. He's 15.

These are my grandparents. My grandfather is 74. My grandmother is 67.

My name is Sonia. I'm 13.

This is my cousin, Mitch. He's 13, like me.

These are my parents. My father is 50. His name is Ned. My mother is 46. Her name is Claire.

This is my uncle, Ron, and my aunt, Sheila. He's 39 and she's 38.

B Complete these sentences about Sonia's family.

1. Sonia's __mother__ is 46.
2. Her father is _____ .
3. Her _____ is 13.
4. Her aunt is _____ .
5. Her _____ is 15.
6. Her sister is _____ .
7. Her _____ are 67 and 74.
8. Her _____ is 39.

UNIT 5 Family and Home

3 Language focus

A Meet Sonia's cousin. Listen and practice.

I'm Mitch. I'm Sonia's cousin. Sonia has a brother and a sister, so I have three cousins. But I have no brothers or sisters – I'm an only child.

have / has

I **have** three cousins.
I **have** no brothers or sisters.
She **has** a brother and a sister.
He **has** no brothers.

cousin → cousins
child → children

B Complete the sentences with *have* or *has*. Then listen and check.

My name is Ron. I'm Sonia's uncle. I <u>have</u> one sister. Her name is Claire. She's Sonia's mother. She _____ three children – Jen, Eddie, and Sonia. I _____ one child, Mitch.

I'm Sonia's grandmother. I _____ two children – Claire and Ron. Claire _____ three children. Ron _____ one child.

4 Speaking

A Complete the information for yourself. Write numbers. Then complete the information about a classmate.

Relative	You
brother(s)	_____
sister(s)	_____
cousin(s)	_____
aunt(s)	_____
uncle(s)	_____

I have two brothers.

I have no brothers.

Relative	Classmate
brother(s)	_____
sister(s)	_____
cousin(s)	_____
aunt(s)	_____
uncle(s)	_____

B Tell the class one thing about you and your classmate.

I have two brothers. Maria has no brothers.

Family and Home 59

Lesson 18 Family reunion

1 Vocabulary

A Read about Sally's family. Then listen and practice.

B Read about Sally's family again. What words describe the people? Write the words in the correct columns.

Appearance	Personality
handsome	friendly

2 Language focus

A Sally and Dan talk about her family. Complete the conversation. Listen and check. Then practice.

> **What's . . . like?**
> **What's** Pam **like?**
> She's **shy**.

Sally That's Pam. She's my cousin.
Dan What's she like?
Sally She's shy and . . .
Dan She's very pretty.
Sally Yes, I know, Dan.
Dan What's your brother _____ ?
Sally Tom? Oh, _____ smart.
Dan And your Aunt Edna? _____ she _____ ?
Sally Well, _____ really funny and a little _____ , too!

B Complete the chart about two members of your family. Then answer a classmate's questions about those family members.

Family member	Appearance	Personality
sister	tall	shy

Sister.   What's your sister like?   She's tall and shy.

3 Pronunciation Final y

Listen to the final *y* in these words. Circle the word that sounds different. Then listen again and practice.

craz**y**   funn**y**   prett**y**   sh**y**   friendl**y**   reall**y**

4 Listening

A What else is true about Sally's family? Listen and match the two parts of each sentence.

1. Sally's mother is tall and ____   a. funny.
2. Sally's cousin, Henry, is handsome and ____   b. a little crazy.
3. Sally's grandfather is friendly and ____   c. thin.
4. Sally's father is short and really ____   d. smart.

B Now ask and answer questions about Sally's family.

What's Sally's mother like?   She's tall and . . . .

Lessons 17 & 18 — Mini-review

1 Language check

A Write the numbers.

1. 31 _thirty-one_
2. 45 _____
3. 100 _____
4. 53 _____
5. 78 _____
6. 24 _____
7. 96 _____
8. 60 _____
9. 82 _____
10. 27 _____
11. 33 _____
12. 86 _____

B Correct the sentences about Jordan's family.

Name	Age	Who?
Jordan	12	me!
Lori	49	mother
Chris	52	father
Jill	15	sister
Jeremiah	24	brother

1. Jordan has ~~no brothers~~ *one brother*.
2. His father is 55.
3. Jacob is his father.
4. His brother is 42.
5. Jill is his aunt.
6. His uncle is 49.

C Nicole talks to Yoshi about her family. Complete the sentences with *have* or *has*.

I _have_ a very big family. I _____ four sisters and three brothers. My mother _____ three brothers, too. My father _____ no brothers, but he _____ five sisters. I _____ 18 cousins. It's great!

D Compare your family to Nicole's family. Tell your classmates.

> Nicole has four sisters. I have no sisters.

2 Listening

A Now listen to Nicole describe three members of her family. Label the photos.

☐ Robert   ☐ Andrew   ☐ John

_____   _____   _____

B Complete the chart with information about three members of your family. Then tell your classmates.

Name	Family member	Age	Description
Peter	cousin	16	tall, thin, very smart

> My cousin's name is Peter. He's 16. He's . . .

Go to page 118 for the Game.

Family and Home

Lesson 19: My new city

1 Vocabulary

A Look at the words in the photos. Listen and practice.

B Tyler's friend Mary lives in San Francisco now. Look at the photos, and complete the sentences about her new neighborhood.

1. ✓ noisy
2. ✓ quiet
3. ✓ big
4. ☐ small
5. ✓ old
6. ☐ new
7. ✓ happy
8. ☐ sad

Dear Tyler,
　San Francisco is great, but it's really __noisy__. My neighborhood isn't noisy – it's nice and very __quiet__. Across the street is a park. Next to my apartment is a __big__ mall with a lot of stores. Behind the mall is a _____ store with cool things.
　My school is really nice. It's very __old__. But inside, the computers, desks, and classrooms are _____.
　I'm really __happy__ in San Francisco. But sometimes I'm _____ – I miss my friends a lot!

　　　　Write soon!
　　　　Mary

C Tell your classmates about your neighborhood.

> My neighborhood is quiet.

2 Language focus

We're / They're; Our / Their

We're happy for you.
They're from Canada.

Our neighbors are very nice.
Their last name is Martel.

We're = We are   They're = They are

Tyler sends a postcard to Mary. Complete Tyler's postcard with *we're, they're, our,* or *their*. Listen and check. Then practice.

Dear Mary,

Thanks for the letter. We miss you, too. But ___we're___ happy for you. San Francisco is a great city.

The Martels live in your house now. _____ from Canada. _____ family is big. _____ all very nice. Nicole Martel and I are in ___Our___ English teacher is her father, Mr. Martel!

Nicole is also on my basketball team. _____ team is really _____ number one! Two players are from Brazil. _____ names are Carlos and Sergio. _____ really good.

Write soon. I miss you a lot!

Tyler

Mary Clark
123 Park Lane
San Francisco, CA 94109

3 Listening

A The Martels talk about where they live. Listen and check (✓) the correct words.

1. the city	☐ nice	✓ big	✓ noisy
2. the neighborhood	☐ pretty	☐ quiet	☐ small
3. the neighbors	☐ happy	☐ quiet	☐ friendly
4. the house	☐ small	☐ nice	☐ new
5. the school	☐ big	☐ small	☐ noisy

B Now compare where you live to where the Martels live. Write three sentences.

Their city is big. Our city is small.

1. _____
2. _____
3. _____

Family and Home

Lesson 20 At home

1 Vocabulary

A Which room is Brandon in? Listen and write the numbers.

B Listen and check. Then practice.

C Where are these things? Answer the questions.

1. Where are Brandon's posters? _They're in the bedroom._
2. Where is his bicycle? _____
3. Where are his comic books? _____
4. Where is his backpack? _____
5. Where is his hat? _____
6. Where are his shoes? _____

2 Language focus

A Match the homes to the correct texts. Listen and check. Then practice.

> **It has . . .**
> **It has** a small yard.
> **It has** three bedrooms.

☐ This is my grandparents' house. It's in the country. It has three bedrooms. It has a small yard.

☐ Our apartment is small, but it's very nice. It has two bedrooms and one bathroom. It has a big kitchen and a nice living room.

☐ My friend has a very big house. It has five bedrooms and three bathrooms! It also has a big garage.

B What's your home like? Write sentences with *It's* and *It has*.

_____

_____

_____

_____

3 Speaking

A What's your dream home like? Check (✓) your ideas.

My dream home is . . .
☐ a house.
☐ an apartment.

It's . . .
☐ in the city.
☐ in the country.

It's . . .
☐ big.
☐ small.

It has . . .
☐ a living room.
☐ a dining room.
☐ bathroom(s).
☐ bedroom(s).

It has . . . , too.
☐ a yard
☐ a garage
☐ a kitchen
☐ a/an _____

The neighborhood is . . .
☐ noisy.
☐ quiet.
☐ nice.

B Now tell your classmates.

> My dream home is a house. It's in the country. It's . . .

Family and Home

Get Connected
UNIT 5

Read

A Read the article quickly. Check (✓) the words you find.

☐ 1. brothers ☐ 3. cousins ☐ 5. parents ☐ 7. fathers
☐ 2. aunts ☐ 4. mother ☐ 6. grandparents ☐ 8. sisters

A Very Big Family

Williams family is very big. Mary and George Williams have 11 children – 7 girls and 4 boys. The **youngest** is Mina. She's six. The **oldest** is Elizabeth. She's 35. Elizabeth lives in a **Different** city and she has a little girl. Bernard, the oldest boy, also lives in a different city and has a little boy. So, Mary and George are parents and grandparents now. Elizabeth's and Bernard's children are **lucky** – they have a lot of aunts and uncles. What about the children still at home? They're not just brothers and sisters, but friends and classmates, too. They go to school together in their house – they're **homeschooled**. Their mother is their teacher. They really like sports. They **run**, play soccer, and play volleyball together. They're a big, happy family.

Go to page 124 for the Vocabulary Practice.

B Read the article slowly. Check your answers in Part A.

C Are these statements true or false? Write *True* or *False*. Then correct the false statements.

1. The family's last name is Foster. *False.* *The family's last name is Heppner.*
2. The oldest sister is 35. _____
3. Mina lives in a different city. _____
4. Elizabeth's and Bernard's children aren't lucky. _____
5. The Williams children's school is their home. _____
6. The Williams family likes sports. _____

68 Unit 5

Twelve cousins!

A 🔘 **Matt and Dave talk about their families. Listen and circle the correct words.**

1. Dave has a really (friendly / small /(big)) family.
2. Dave has (twelve / seven / nine) cousins.
3. Dave is (a grandfather / a father / an uncle).
4. Matt has (two cousins and one sister / three aunts or uncles / a small family).
5. Matt's house is (noisy / quiet / crazy).

B Complete the sentences so they are true for you.

1. I think big families are _____ .
2. I think small families are _____ .
3. I have _____ brothers and / or sisters. I think _____ .
4. I have _____ aunts and / or uncles. I think _____ .

Your turn

A Complete the web.

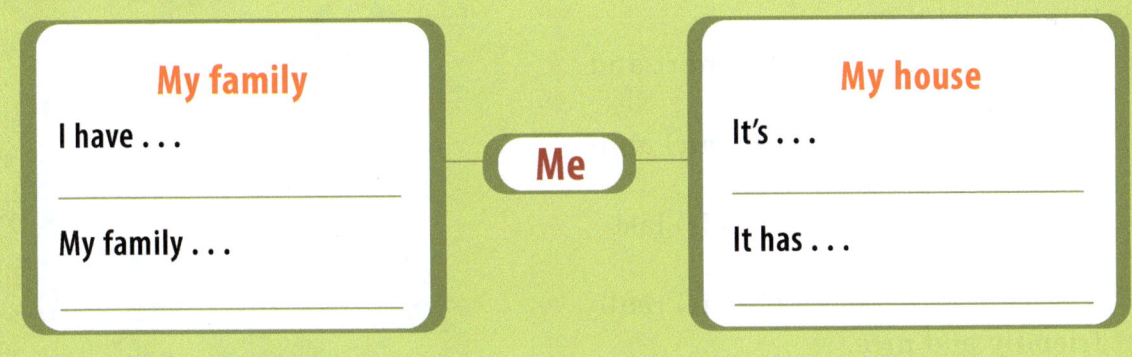

B Write about your family and your house. Use the web in Part A to help you.

I have _____

Family and Home 69

Unit 5 Review

Language chart review

has / have statements	We're / They're; Our / Their	What's ... like?
I **have** two sisters. I **have** no brothers. He **has** a big family. She **has** an apartment. It **has** one bedroom.	**We're** from New York. **Our** last name is Diaz. **They're** from Chicago. **Their** last name is Carlton. We're = We are They're = They are	**What's** she **like**? She's **nice**.

A Complete the conversation.

Farah This is a picture of ___our___ (we / our) family.
Diego You and Paul _____ (have / has) a big family.
Farah Yeah. We _____ (have / has) a lot of brothers and sisters.
Diego Who's this?
Paul This is _____ (we / our) brother, Kyle.
Diego What's he like?
Paul _____ (He's / His) smart and a little shy.
Farah This is _____ (we / our) aunt, Carmen, and uncle, Larry.
Paul _____ (They're / Their) last name is Parsons.
Farah _____ (They're / Their) really friendly and nice.
Paul _____ (They're / Their) from Texas.
Diego I'm from Arizona.
Farah _____ (We're / Our) from Arizona, too!

B Read the conversation again. Answer these questions.

1. What's their brother like? _____
2. What are their aunt and uncle like? _____
3. Where is their uncle from? _____
4. Where are Farah and Paul from? _____

C Complete the sentences with the words in the box.

☐ her ☐ his ☑ my ☐ my ☐ our ☐ their ☐ your

I'm Johnny Martin. This is __my__ father. _____ name is Cal. _____ mother's name is Kimberly. I have one sister. _____ name is Nicki. I have two brothers, too. _____ names are Darren and Leo. _____ family is pretty big. What's _____ family like?

D Write about your family. Use some of the words from Part C.

I'm . . .

E What's the difference? Compare Amy's house and Ben's house. Write sentences with *has* and *has no*.

Amy's house
Kitchen, Living room, Bedroom, Dining room, Bedroom, Bathroom, Bedroom, Bathroom

Ben's house
Garage, Kitchen, Living room, Bedroom, Bathroom, Bedroom

1. (bedroom) Amy's house has three bedrooms.
   Ben's house has two bedrooms.
2. (living room) _____
3. (bathroom) _____
4. (dining room) _____
5. (kitchen) _____
6. (garage) _____

Go to page 130 for the Theme Project.

Family and Home 71

Lesson 21: The media center

1 Vocabulary

A Look at the picture of the new media center and write the names of the items. Use the words in the box. Then listen and practice.

☑ board ☐ cabinet ☐ printer ☐ scanner
☐ bookcase ☐ CD/DVD player ☐ remote control ☐ screen

1. _____
2. _____
3. _____
4. _____
5. _____
6. _____
7. _____
8. _____

B Ask and answer questions about things in your classroom.

What's that?   It's a board.   What are those?   They're computers.

UNIT 6 At School

2 Language focus

A There is a problem in the media center. Listen and practice.

> **There's / There are . . .**
> **There's a** printer.
> **There are** six computers.
>
> **There's no / There are no . . .**
> **There's no** wastebasket.
> **There are no** chairs.
>
> There's = There is

Mr. Wilson So, here's the new media center.
Ms. Brooks Wow! It's great.
Mr. Wilson Wait a minute . . .
There's a problem.
Ms. Brooks What's wrong?
Mr. Wilson Well, there are only six computers.
Ms. Brooks Oh, dear. Well, there's a printer. Is that right?
Mr. Wilson Yes, that's OK. But there's no wastebasket, and there are no chairs.
Ms. Brooks Oh, no!

Mr. Wilson
Clarkston Middle School

☐ 2 boards ☐ 1 CD/DVD player ✓ 1 printer
☐ 2 bookcases ☐ 8 chairs ☐ 1 screen
☐ 2 cabinets ✓ 8 computers ☐ 1 scanner
☐ 1 remote control ☐ 8 desks ☐ 1 wastebasket

B Look at Mr. Wilson's order form in Exercise 2A. Then look at the picture on page 72. What's right? What's wrong? Write sentences. Then listen and check.

What's right?	What's wrong?
There's a printer.	There are six computers.

3 Speaking

Make true or false statements about your classroom. Your classmate says *Yes* or *No* and corrects the false statements.

You There's a board.
Classmate Yes.
You There are 12 chairs.
Classmate No. There are 20 chairs.

At School 73

Lesson 22 — Around school

1 Vocabulary

A Label the photos of Jenny's school with the words in the brochure. Then listen and practice.

Kent International School Has A Lot!

1. gym

Sports Facilities
- 2 tennis courts
- 4 athletic fields
  * 1 football field
  * 1 baseball field
  * 2 soccer fields
- gym
- swimming pool

Media Center
- computer lab with 50 computers
- language lab

Other Facilities
- auditorium
- library
- cafeteria

B Write about the facilities at your school. Use *There is / There are*.

There is ...

2 Language focus

A Jenny's cousin, Jill, asks about Kent International School. Listen and practice.

Jill Jenny, your school is really great. Are there any tennis courts?
Jenny Yes, there are. There's a tennis team, too.
Jill So, are there any cute players?
Jenny No, there aren't.
Jill Hmm. Is there a soccer team?
Jenny Yes, there is.
Jill Is there a game today?
Jenny No, there isn't. Sorry.

> **Is there a / Are there any . . . ?**
>
> **Is there a** soccer team?
>   Yes, **there is**.
>   No, **there isn't**.
> **Are there any** tennis courts?
>   Yes, **there are**.
>   No, **there aren't**.
>
> isn't = is not   aren't = are not

B Complete the rest of the conversation. Listen and check. Then practice.

Jill __Are__ there any other interesting things at your school?
Jenny Yes, there _____ . There are some new classrooms and a new media center.
Jill Oh, that's cool. _____ there an Internet café there?
Jenny No, there _____ .
Jill Hey, I'm hungry. Are there _____ cafés near here?
Jenny No, there _____ . But there's a cafeteria.
Jill Are _____ any cute boys there?
Jenny Yes, there _____ . Let's go!

3 Pronunciation *th*

A Listen to the two pronunciations of *th*. Then listen again and practice.

Voiced	Unvoiced
there **th**at fa**th**er	**th**ree **th**ink ba**th**room

B Write these words in the correct columns: *birthday, brother, mother, thanks, the, they, thing, thirty*. Listen and check. Then practice.

Voiced	Unvoiced
_____	_____
_____	_____
_____	_____
_____	_____

At School 75

Lessons 21 & 22 Mini-review

1 Language check

A Read about the neighborhood around Kent International School. Then answer the questions.

Enjoy your free time after school!

Bob's Burgers
Hamburgers, sandwiches, and more!
325 Main Street
555-0982

Kent Shopping Mall
48 stores,
5 movie theaters
25 Park Avenue
555-1618

Central Park
56th–60th Streets
Swimming pool
Soccer and baseball fields

Lee's Restaurant
Great Chinese food!
16 West Avenue
555-6723

City Video Arcade
Your place for after-school fun!
18 South Avenue
555-8722

Maple Bookstore and Internet Café
New and used books
Kent Shopping Mall
555-8655

1. Are there any stores near the school? _Yes, there are._
2. Are there any athletic fields in the neighborhood? _____
3. Is there a basketball court in the park? _____
4. Is there a bookstore at the mall? _____
5. Are there any restaurants on South Avenue? _____
6. Is there a video arcade in the neighborhood? _____

B Write three sentences about your neighborhood. Then tell your classmates.

There's a park.

1. _____
2. _____
3. _____

There's a park. There . . .

C Look at the picture. Circle the correct words to complete the sentences.

1. There's a (cabinet / (wastebasket)) next to the desk.
2. There's a large (computer / board) on the desk.
3. There's a (scanner / CD/DVD player) under the desk.
4. There's a (remote control / screen) next to the CD/DVD player.
5. There are no (chairs / pencils) near the desk.
6. There's a (bookcase / printer) next to the computer.

2 Listening

People talk about their schools. Listen and answer the questions.
Write the correct information for *No* answers.

1. Are there two scanners in the media center? <u>No, there aren't. There's one scanner.</u>
2. Are the answers on the screen? _____
3. Are there five wastebaskets in the classroom? _____
4. Is there a football field at Jim's school? _____
5. Are there three swimming pools at Mia's school? _____
6. Are there 20 computers in the computer lab? _____

At School 77

Lesson 23 — School subjects

1 Vocabulary

A These are some of the classes at Kent International School. Label the books with the words in the box. Then listen and practice.

☐ art ☐ geography ☐ history ☐ music ☐ science
☐ English ☐ health ☐ math ☑ physical education (P.E.) ☐ Spanish

B Make a list of your school subjects. Are they easy or difficult for you? Check (✓) *Easy* or *Difficult*. Then tell your classmates.

My school subjects	Easy	Difficult
_____	☐	☐
_____	☐	☐
_____	☐	☐
_____	☐	☐
_____	☐	☐

My school subjects	Easy	Difficult
_____	☐	☐
_____	☐	☐
_____	☐	☐
_____	☐	☐
_____	☐	☐

I think geography is *easy*.

I think math is *difficult*.

2 Saying the time

Look at the days and times in Nicole's class schedule.
Listen and practice.

Saying the time
8:30 = eight thirty
1:05 = one-oh-five
2:00 = two or two o'clock

Class Schedule for _Nicole Martel_

	Monday	Tuesday	Wednesday	Thursday	Friday
8:30	English	English	English	English	English
9:25	math	math	math	computer lab	math
10:20	P.E.	health	P.E.	art	P.E.
11:15	lunch	lunch	lunch	lunch	lunch
12:10	history	geography	history	geography	history
1:05	science	science	science lab	science	science
2:00	Spanish	language lab	Spanish	music	Spanish

3 Language focus

A Nicole talks about her class schedule.
Listen and practice.

on / at
I have computer lab **on** Thursday.
My computer lab is **at** 9:25.

This is my school schedule. I have English class every day at 8:30. I think English is easy.

I have history class at 12:10 on Monday, Wednesday, and Friday. History is difficult.

My favorite day is Thursday. I have computer lab at 9:25. It's great!

B Look at Nicole's class schedule in Exercise 2 above. Complete the sentences with the day and time. Then listen and check.

1. Nicole's health class is _on Tuesday at 10:20_ .
2. Nicole has science lab _____ .
3. Her geography class is _____ .
4. She has Spanish class _____ .
5. Her language lab is _____ .

4 Speaking

What are your three favorite classes at school? When are they?
Tell your classmates.

I think math is great. I have math class on Tuesday at 1:00. I think . . .

Lesson 24 — Spring Day

1 Vocabulary

A Look at the Spring Day poster. Listen and practice.

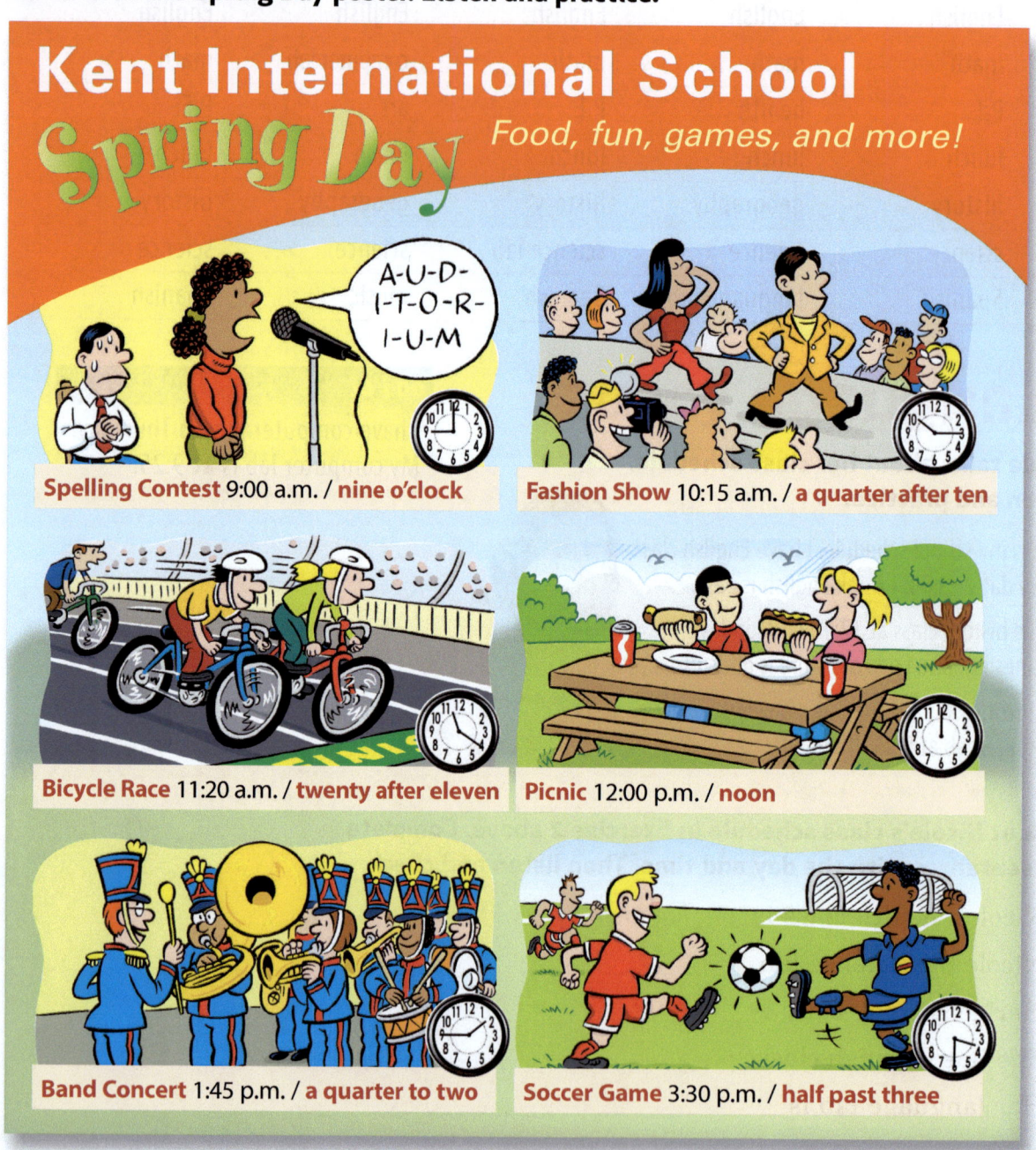

B What time are the events? Complete the sentences.

1. The _____ is at a quarter after ten.
2. The picnic is at _____ .
3. The soccer game is at _____ .

2 Language focus

A Yoshi and Paulo are at Spring Day. Listen and practice.

Yoshi Are you excited about Spring Day?
Paulo Yes, I am. I'm in the spelling contest and the soccer game.
Yoshi Uh, what time is the spelling contest?
Paulo It's at nine o'clock. What time is it now?
Yoshi It's five minutes after nine.
Paulo Oh, no! I'm already late.

> **What time . . . ?**
> **What time** is it now?
> **It's** 9:05. (It's nine-oh-five.)
> **It's** five (minutes) after nine.
> **What time** is the spelling contest?
> **It's** at nine (o'clock).

B It's Spring Day at another International School. Write questions and answers. Then listen and check.

1. (bicycle race) <u>What time is the bicycle race?</u>
   (10:15) <u>It's at a quarter after ten.</u>

2. (fashion show) _____
   (3:30) _____

3. (band concert) _____
   (12:20) _____

4. (picnic) _____
   (1:15) _____

5. (soccer game) _____
   (2:45) _____

3 Listening

What time is it now? Listen and check (✓) the correct time.

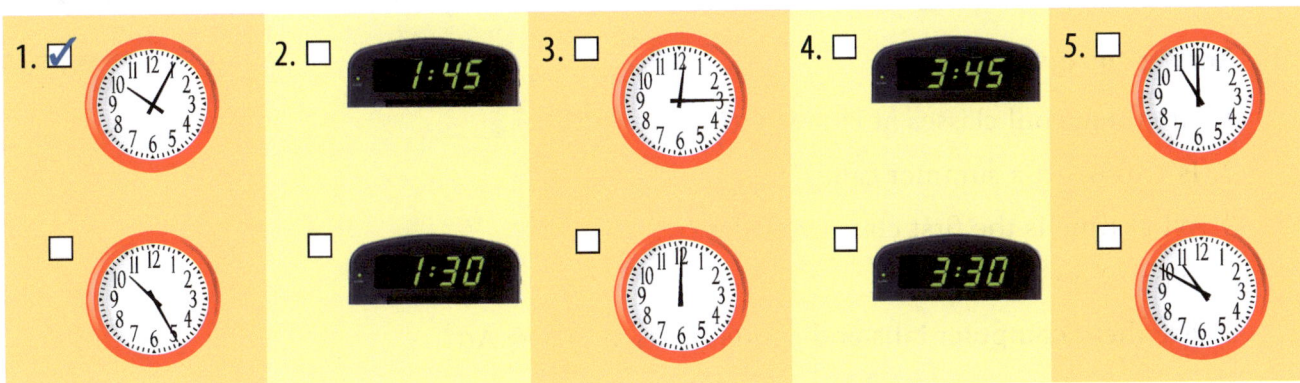

Get Connected
UNIT 6

Read

A Read the information quickly. Check (✓) the times you find.

☐ 12:30 ☐ 3:30 ☐ 9:15
☐ 9:00   ☐ 3:15 ☐ 12:30

Welcome to Kiowa U!

Every **summer**, kids (ages 7–16) from around the world go to Fun & Art in Denton, Texas. At Fun & Art, there are cool classes in **3D animation, fashion design, cooking** – and a lot of other classes, too. Is Fun & Art a school? No, it's a **summer camp**!

What time are classes every day? Well, students have their first class at 9:00 a.m., and they have lunch at 12:30 p.m. They have other classes at 3:15 p.m. – soccer, basketball, **juggling** . . . At 7:00 p.m., students go to the movies, go bowling, play games, have talent shows . . . It's everybody's favorite time of day.

Are there any classrooms at Fun & Art? Yes, there are, and there are also computer labs, a gym, a swimming pool, and sports fields. Kiowa U has a lot of things. It's great!

Go to page 124 for the **Vocabulary Practice**.

B Read the article slowly. Check your answers in Part A.

C Answer the questions.

1. Are there cool classes at Fun & Art? _Yes, there are._
2. Is Fun & Art a summer camp? _____
3. What time is the first class every day? _____
4. What time is lunch? _____
5. Are there computer labs and sports fields at Fun & Art? _____

What time is the game?

A Elsa and Chris talk about summer camp. Listen and write *True* or *False*. Then correct the false statements.

1. Chris is excited about summer camp. _False._   _Chris isn't excited about summer camp._
2. Chris has science class at 10:00. _____ _____
3. Chris has P.E. at summer camp. _____ _____
4. There's a gym at Chris's summer camp. _____ _____
5. The basketball game is at 3:30 on Saturday. _____ _____
6. The picnic is at noon on Saturday. _____ _____

B Complete the statements so they are true for you.

1. I think summer camp is _____ .
2. I think math and English classes in the summer are _____ .
3. I think basketball is _____ .
4. I think picnics with friends are _____ .

Your turn

Write

A Think about your dream summer camp. Answer the questions about it.

1. What's the name of your summer camp? _____
2. Where is it? _____
3. What's at the camp? A swimming pool? A sports field? A computer lab? _____
   _____
4. What's the schedule every day? _____

B Write about your dream summer camp. Use the answers in Part A to help you.

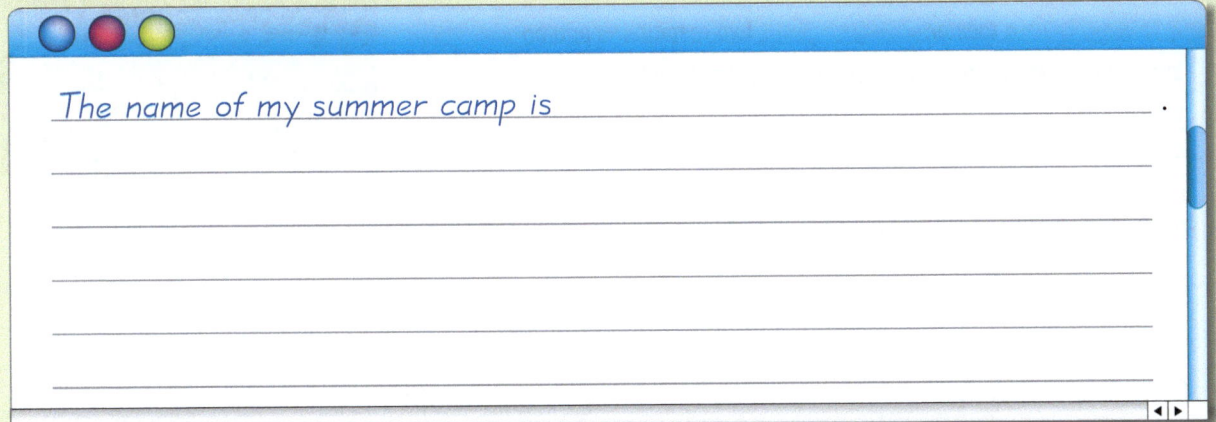

The name of my summer camp is _____ .

At School 83

Unit 6 Review

Language chart review

There's / There are

There's a nice library in my neighborhood.
There are two athletic fields at my school.

There's no library in my neighborhood.
There are no athletic fields at my school.

Is there a / Are there any . . . ?

Is there a park in your neighborhood?
   Yes, there is.
   No, there isn't.

Are there any restaurants in your neighborhood?
   Yes, there are.
   No, there aren't.

There's = There is   isn't = is not   aren't = are not

A Complete the e-mails with *there's*, *there are*, *there's no*, and *there are no*.

From: Claudia
Hi, Terri!
Here's a picture of my city – Rio de Janeiro, Brazil. <u>There are</u> many interesting places here. Rio has a lot of beaches. My favorite beach is Copacabana Beach. _____ a famous mountain here, too. It's Sugar Loaf. _____ a theater downtown. It's the Municipal Theater. _____ many concerts at the theater. The National Museum of Fine Arts is famous. It's a great city. I love it!
Come visit me soon!
Claudia

From: Terri
Dear Claudia,
Thanks for your e-mail. Rio is beautiful. My town is very small. _____ museum here. _____ beaches here. _____ a theater. _____ two restaurants and an Internet café. My town is a little boring, but I like it a lot!
Bye!
Terri

B Write questions and answers about Terri's town.

1. (a museum) Q: <u>Is there a museum?</u>   A: <u>No, there isn't.</u>
2. (a café) Q: _____   A: _____
3. (any beaches) Q: _____   A: _____
4. (any restaurants) Q: _____   A: _____

Language chart review

What time...?	on / at
What time is it?	I have art **on** Tuesday.
It's ten forty-five.	Lunch is **at** 11:15.
What time is the concert?	There's a soccer game **on** Monday **at** 5:00.
It's at six.	

C Write questions to complete the conversation.

Sandra <u>Is there a volleyball game tonight?</u>

Tyler Yes, there is. There's a volleyball game in the gym.

Sandra _____ ?

Tyler It's at 10:00.

Sandra _____ ?

Tyler Hmm . . . It's 9:45, now.

Sandra Let's hurry!

D Look at the posters and write sentences.

1. <u>There's a concert on Tuesday at eight o'clock.</u>

2. _____

3. _____

4. _____

Go to page 131 for the Theme Project.

At School 85

Lesson 25: People and countries

1 Vocabulary

A English is an official language in over 50 countries. Here are some of the countries. Listen and practice.

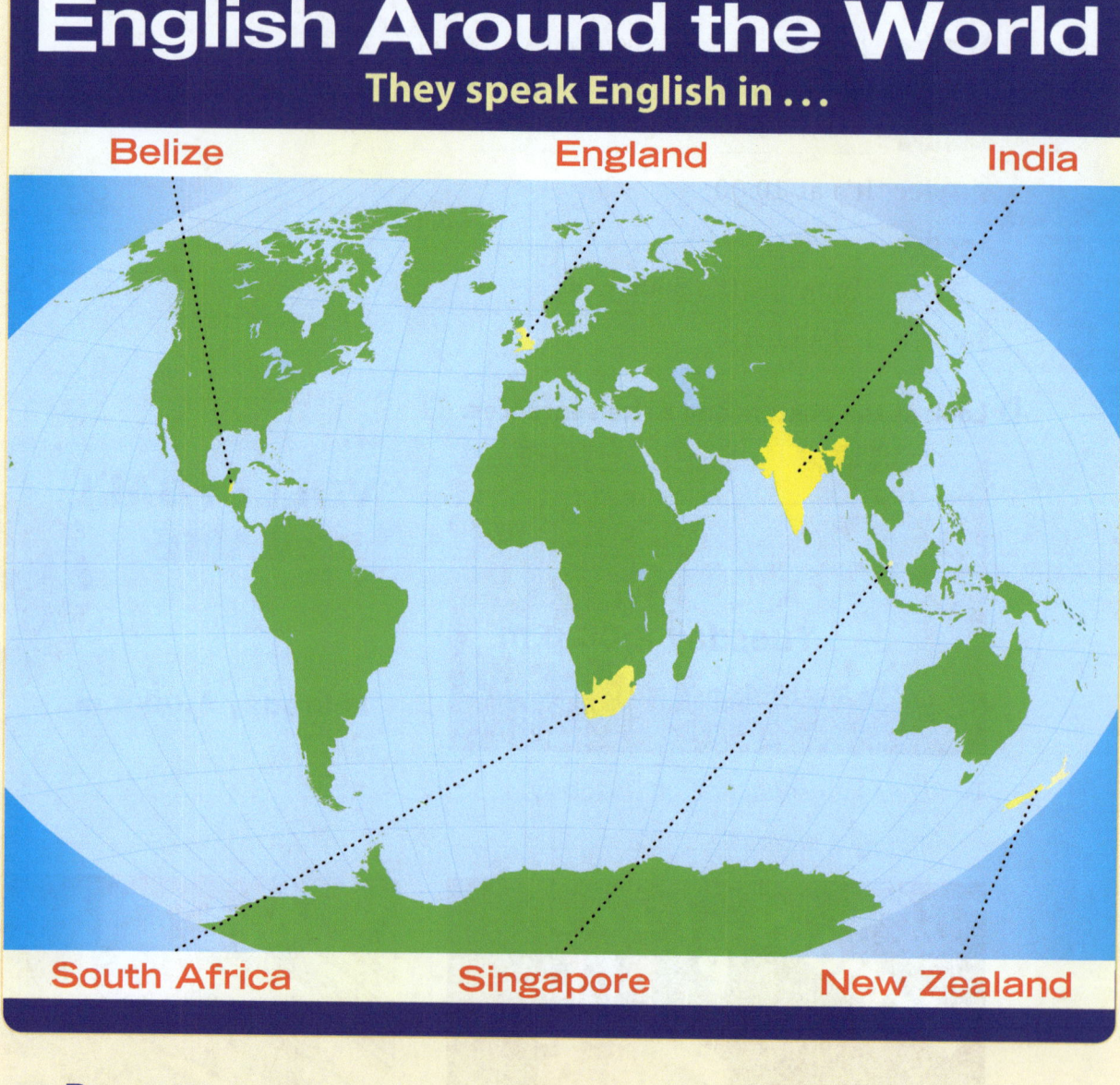

English Around the World
They speak English in ...
- Belize
- England
- India
- South Africa
- Singapore
- New Zealand

B Hannah's parents talk about a world vacation. Listen. Number the countries in the order that the family will visit them.

- ☐ Canada
- ☐ India
- ☐ Belize
- ☐ South Africa
- ☐ England
- ☐ New Zealand
- ☐ Singapore
- [1] the United States

UNIT 7 Around the World

86

2 Language focus

A Hannah shows her vacation photos to Mark. Listen and practice.

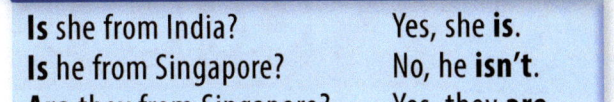

is / isn't; are / aren't in short answers

Is she from India?	Yes, she **is**.
Is he from Singapore?	No, he **isn't**.
Are they from Singapore?	Yes, they **are**.
Are they from New Zealand?	No, they **aren't**.

isn't = is not   aren't = are not

Hannah Here I am with Tom and Bruce.
Mark Are they from England?
Hannah No, they aren't. They're from New Zealand.
Mark Wow! Look at this photo. These girls are very pretty! Are they from Singapore?
Hannah Yes, they are. They have e-mail! I can introduce you.
Mark Great! And this boy? Is he from Singapore, too?
Hannah No, he isn't. He's from India. His name is Ravi. And this is his friend, Usha.
Mark Is she from India, too?
Hannah Yes, she is.
Mark Wow! You have a lot of new friends!
Hannah Yes, and they all speak English!

B Look at Part A. Answer the questions. Then listen and check.

1. Are Tom and Bruce from Canada? _No, they aren't._
2. Is Ravi from India? _____
3. Is Usha from Singapore? _____
4. Are the girls from England? _____
5. Are the girls from Singapore? _____

3 Speaking

Complete the sentences with names of places. A classmate guesses the places.

He's from New Zealand.

He's from _____ .

She's from _____ .

They're from _____ .

Classmate Is he from Belize?
You No, he isn't.
Classmate Is he from New Zealand?
You Yes, he is.

Around the World 87

Lesson 26: Nationalities

1 Vocabulary

A Take the Internet quiz. Match the photos to the correct texts. Then listen and practice.

B Complete the chart with the words in the box. Then listen and practice.

☑ American ☐ Brazilian ☐ Canadian ☐ Japanese ☐ Peruvian ☐ South Korean
☐ Australian ☐ British ☐ French ☐ Mexican ☐ Puerto Rican ☐ Spanish

Place	Nationality
1. the United States	American
2. Japan	
3. Brazil	
4. Spain	
5. England	
6. France	

Place	Nationality
7. South Korea	
8. Australia	
9. Puerto Rico	
10. Peru	
11. Mexico	
12. Canada	

2 Pronunciation — Syllable stress

Listen. Underline the stressed part of each word. Then listen again and practice.

1. Ca <u>na</u> di an
2. <u>Mex</u> i can
3. Ko re an
4. Pe ru vi an
5. Bri tish
6. Jap a nese
7. A mer i can
8. Span ish
9. Puer to Ri can
10. Bra zil ian
11. Aus tral ian
12. Co lom bi an

3 Language focus

Complete the quiz with *isn't* or *aren't*. Who are these stars? Listen and check.

> **isn't / aren't in statements**
> He **isn't** American.
> His movies **aren't** all in English.

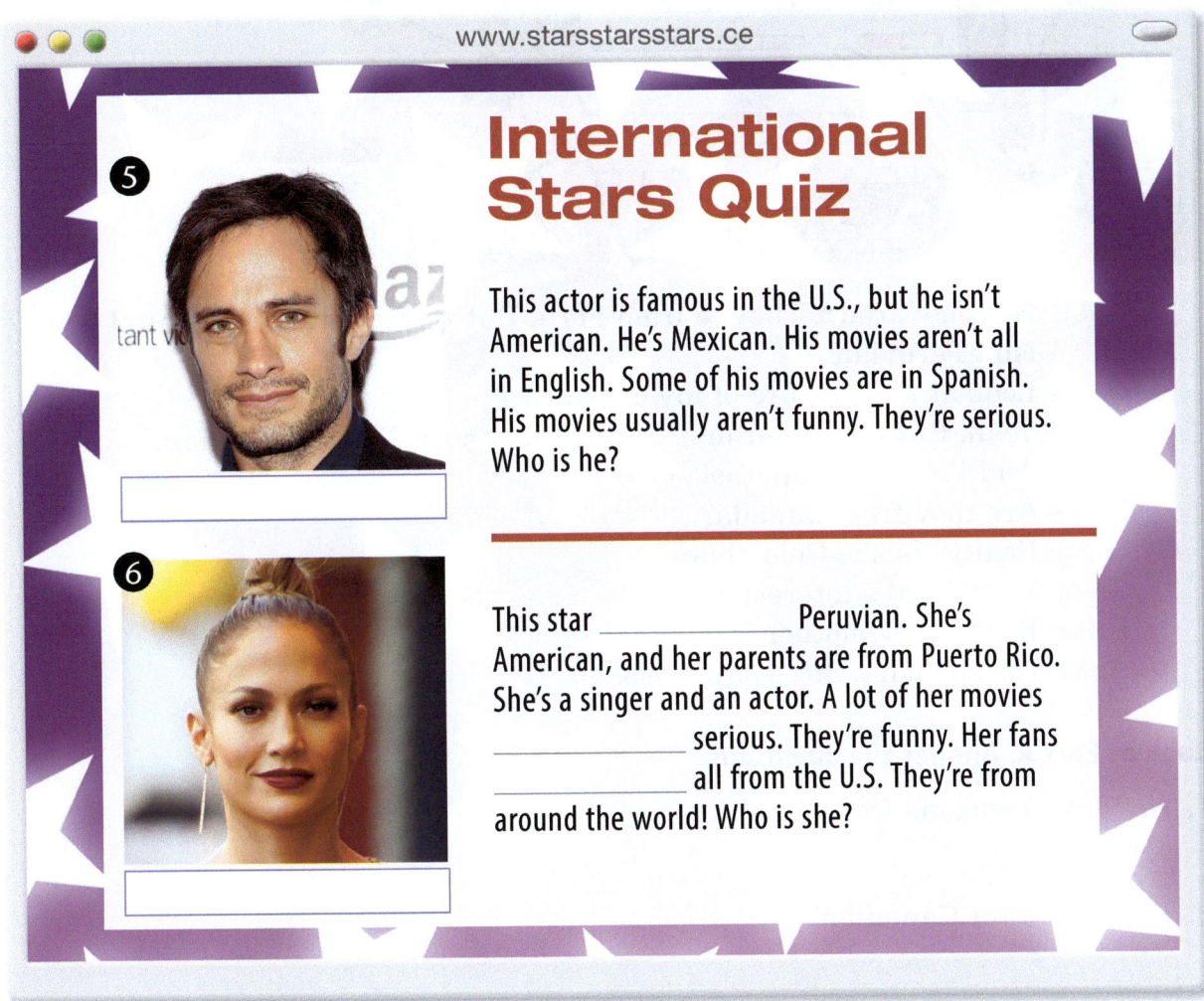

International Stars Quiz

❺ This actor is famous in the U.S., but he isn't American. He's Mexican. His movies aren't all in English. Some of his movies are in Spanish. His movies usually aren't funny. They're serious. Who is he?

❻ This star _____ Peruvian. She's American, and her parents are from Puerto Rico. She's a singer and an actor. A lot of her movies _____ serious. They're funny. Her fans _____ all from the U.S. They're from around the world! Who is she?

4 Speaking

Make false statements about stars to a classmate. Your classmate corrects them.

You Vitor Faverani is British.
Classmate He isn't British. He's Brazilian.

Mini-review

1 Language check

A Number the sentences in the correct order.

___ **Jake** No, they aren't. They're from Peru. But their mother – my aunt – isn't Peruvian.
_1_ **Jake** Look at this picture of my cousins.
___ **Luisa** Yeah. But my father and I aren't Japanese. We're Canadian.
___ **Jake** And I'm Canadian, too!
___ **Luisa** Are they from Canada?
___ **Luisa** Really? Is she Colombian?
___ **Jake** Wow! That's interesting.
___ **Luisa** Really? My mother is Japanese.
___ **Jake** No, she isn't. She's Japanese.

B Look at Part A. Answer the questions.

1. Are Jake's cousins from Peru?
   Yes, they are.

2. Is Jake's aunt Canadian?
   _____

3. Is Luisa's mother Japanese?
   _____

4. Are Luisa and her father Japanese?
   _____

5. Is Jake Canadian?
   _____

90 Unit 7

C Look at Jenny's e-mail address book. Then correct the sentences below.

Full name	City / Place	E-mail addre
Amanda Dart	Sydney, Australia	adat@prest
Mike Maynard	Montreal, Canada	mmaynard@
Emiko Koga	Kyoto, Japan	koga@iscor
Jack Crowe	Melbourne, Australia	jackc@prisr
Juan Rivera	Acapulco, Mexico	jrivera@yal
Peter Stockwell	Vancouver, Canada	Pstock3@c
Claudia Ferreira	São Paulo, Brazil	claferr@spe

1. Emiko is Canadian. *She isn't Canadian. She's Japanese.*
2. Melbourne and Sydney are in Japan. *They aren't . . .*
3. Claudia is from Mexico. _____
4. Juan and Amanda are from Canada. _____
5. Peter is American. _____
6. Kyoto is in Brazil. _____
7. Montreal and Vancouver are in the United States. _____

D Now check your answers with a classmate.

> Is Emiko Canadian?

> No, she isn't. She's Japanese.

2 Listening

A Paulo talks about his e-pals. Listen and check (✓) their nationalities.

1. Lee	☐ South Korean	☐ Puerto Rican
2. Ashley and Helen	☐ Australian	☐ British
3. Alberto	☐ Peruvian	☐ Mexican
4. Angela and Hector	☐ American	☐ Spanish

B Compare answers with a classmate.

> Lee is . . . .

> That's right.

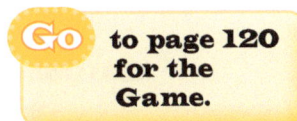

Go to page 120 for the Game.

Lesson 27 Holidays

1 Vocabulary

A Listen and practice the months of the year.

> January February March April May June July
> August September October November December

B When are these holidays in the U.S.? Complete the sentences with the months below. Then listen and practice.

☐ February ☑ May ☐ June ☐ July ☐ November ☐ December

1.
Mother's Day is in __May__.

2.
Thanksgiving is in _____.

3.
Valentine's Day is in _____.

4.
Father's Day is in _____.

5.
Independence Day is in _____.

6.
New Year's Eve is in _____.

C Talk about your favorite holiday with a classmate.

You What's your favorite holiday?
Classmate It's .... It's in .... What's your favorite holiday?
You It's .... It's in ....

2 Language focus

When is . . . ?
When is Independence Day?
It's in July.

A Jenny chats with her e-pal, José. Listen and practice.

Chat with José

José: Jenny, are you online?
Jenny: Yes, I am. How are you, José?
José: I'm great. It's Independence Day in Mexico today. It's a holiday – no school. Yay!
Jenny: Wow, you're lucky. I'm at school right now.
José: When is Independence Day in the U.S.?
Jenny: It's in July. It's my favorite holiday.

B Look at Exercise 1B. Write four questions about holidays in the U.S. Then ask and answer the questions.

<u>When is New Year's Eve?</u>

1. _____
2. _____
3. _____
4. _____

When is New Year's Eve?   It's in December.

3 Listening

A When are these holidays? Listen and match the two parts of each sentence.

1. Independence Day in Mexico is in ____
2. Thanksgiving Day in Canada is in ____
3. Children's Day in Japan is in ____
4. Australia Day is in ____

a. January.
b. May.
c. September.
d. October.

B Ask and answer questions about holidays in your country.

When is Carnaval in Brazil?   It's in February or March.

Around the World   93

Lesson 28 — Important days

1 Vocabulary

A Look at the calendar. Listen and practice the numbers.

March

Sunday	Monday	Tuesday	Wednesday	Thursday	Friday	Saturday
1st first	2nd second	3rd third	4th fourth	5th fifth	6th sixth	7th seventh
8th eighth	9th ninth	10th tenth	11th eleventh	12th twelfth	13th thirteenth	14th fourteenth
15th fifteenth	16th sixteenth	17th seventeenth	18th eighteenth	19th nineteenth	20th twentieth	21st twenty-first
22nd twenty-second	23rd twenty-third	24th twenty-fourth	25th twenty-fifth	26th twenty-sixth	27th twenty-seventh	28th twenty-eighth
29th twenty-ninth	30th thirtieth	31st thirty-first				

B Say these dates. Then listen and practice.

January 1st   April 5th   July 3rd   October 31st
February 22nd   May 17th   August 12th   November 18th
March 13th   June 11th   September 9th   December 24th

2 Listening

Paulo and Nicole make a list of birthdays. Listen and complete the chart.

Name	Birthday
Sandra	September twelfth
Jenny	
Tyler	
Yoshi	
Nicole	
Paulo	

94 Unit 7

3 Language focus

A Daryl and Kimberly are e-pals. They write about their favorite months. Listen and practice.

> **in / on**
> The first day of school is **in September**.
> My best friend's birthday is **on September 28th**.

The first day of school is in September. And my best friend's birthday is on September 28th. He has great parties. I'm always happy in September.

Daryl
Dallas, U.S.

My favorite month is December. The last day of school is on December 22nd. My birthday is on December 31st. There are a lot of holidays in December, too.

Kimberly
Auckland, New Zealand

B Complete the sentences with *in* or *on*. For items 5 and 6, use your own information. Then listen and check.

1. There are a lot of holidays __in__ November.
2. Valentine's Day is _____ February 14th.
3. Father's Day is _____ June.
4. Independence Day in the U.S. is _____ July 4th.
5. My last day of school is _____ .
6. My best friend's birthday is _____ .

4 Speaking

Ask four classmates about their birthdays. Then complete the chart.

You When's your birthday?
Classmate It's on . . . .

Classmate	Birthday

Around the World 95

Get Connected
UNIT 7

Read

A Read the article quickly. Check (✓) the statements that are true.

☐ 1. It's everyone's birthday on the first day of the New Year's celebration in Thailand.
☐ 2. Children throw water out the window on New Year's Eve in Puerto Rico.
☐ 3. The famous New Year's ball goes down in Times Square on New Year's Eve.

New Year's Fun Around the World

The New Year's holiday is **important** around the world. There are some interesting **celebrations**, but they aren't only on January 1.

In Vietnam, the New Year's celebration is in February and everyone's birthday is on the first day of that celebration! Children **receive** money from their families and good friends. The money is very lucky.

In Thailand, the New Year's celebration is on April 15. Everyone **throws** water on their friends for good luck. Puerto Rican children throw water, too. They throw it out the **window** at 12:00 a.m. on New Year's Eve (December 31). It's really fun – and lucky!

On New Year's Eve, a lot of people in the U.S. watch the famous New Year's ball go down in Times Square in New York City. It's really cool! When is the New Year's holiday in your country?

Go to page 125 for the Vocabulary Practice.

B Read the article slowly. Check your answers in Part A.

C Answer the questions.

1. When is everyone's birthday in Vietnam? <u>Everyone's birthday is in February.</u>
2. What's lucky for children in Vietnam to receive on New Year's? _____
3. When is the New Year's celebration in Thailand? _____
4. In Puerto Rico, when is it lucky to throw water out the window? _____
5. Where's the famous New Year's ball in the U.S.? _____

It's in January or February.

A Andy and Kim talk about holidays. Listen and answer the questions.

1. Is Ming Chinese? _Yes, he is._
2. When is Chinese New Year? _____
3. Is Ming excited? _____
4. What's Kim's favorite day? _____
5. What time is the party? _____

B Complete the sentences so they are true for you.

1. I think New Year's Day is _____ in my country.
2. I think Valentine's Day is _____ .
3. Birthday parties are _____ .
4. Holidays with families and friends are _____ .

Your turn

A Complete the chart about holidays in your country.

	When is it?	What's the holiday like?
What's an important holiday? _____		
What's your favorite holiday? _____		
What's a boring holiday? _____		

B Write about the three holidays. Use the chart in Part A to help you.

_____ is a very important holiday in my country.
It's on / in _____ . _____
_____
_____

Around the World

Unit 7 Review

Language chart review

isn't / aren't in statements	isn't / aren't in short answers	Questions with when in / on
She **isn't** American. They **aren't** French.	**Is she** American? Yes, **she is**. No, **she isn't**. **Are they** Peruvian? Yes, **they are**. No, **they aren't**.	**When is** Bobby's birthday? It's **in** June. It's **on** June 2nd.

A Read the article. Then answer the questions.

1. Is Shakira from Brazil? <u>No, she isn't.</u>
2. Is Hee-Seop a soccer player? _____
3. Are Abigail and Marion actors? _____
4. Is Wagner Brazilian? _____
5. Are Shakira and Marion's birthdays in August? _____
6. Is Wagner's birthday in June? _____

B Look at Part A. Write about two people.

<u>Shakira is a singer. She's Colombian.</u>
<u>Her birthday is on February 2nd.</u>

1. _____

2. _____

C Look at Pauline's calendar. Write a question for each answer.

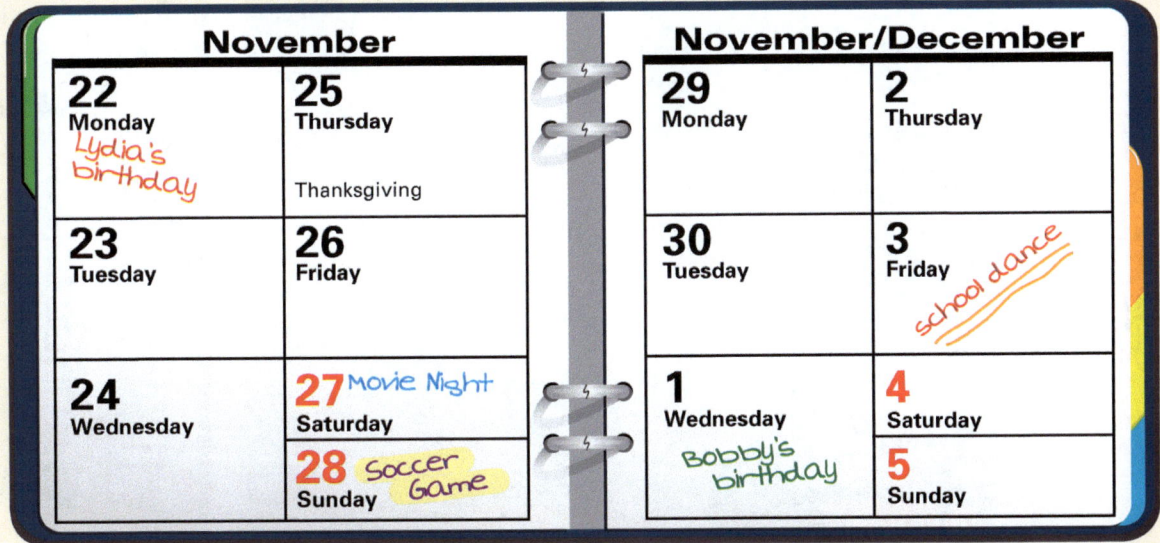

1. Q: <u>When is the school dance?</u> A: It's on December 3rd.
2. Q: _____ A: It's on November 25th.
3. Q: _____ A: It's on November 27th.
4. Q: _____ A: It's on December 1st.

D Look at Pauline's calendar again. Correct the sentences with *isn't* and *aren't*. Spell out the numbers.

1. Lydia's birthday is on November 23rd. <u>Lydia's birthday isn't on November twenty-third. It's on November twenty-second.</u>

2. The soccer game and movie night are in December. _____

3. Movie night is November 28th. _____

4. The school dance is on December 1st. _____

5. Bobby's birthday is in November. _____

Go to page 132 for the Theme Project.

Around the World

Lesson 29: Favorite places

1 Vocabulary

A These are three students' favorite places. Match the photos to the correct texts. Then listen and practice.

1. beach

2. zoo

3. wax museum

☐ This place is in Singapore. It's *interesting*. It's not *boring*. There are animals from around the world here. There are kangaroos from Australia in this place.

☐ This place is in Los Angeles. It's *fun*, but it's always *crowded*. There are wax models of famous actors. There's even a model of Harrison Ford as Indiana Jones.

☐ This place is in Mazatlán, Mexico. It's *beautiful*. It's really *exciting*, too. It's my favorite place for a vacation.

B Read the words. What places do you think of? Complete the chart and then tell your classmates.

Word	Place		Word	Place
beautiful	Ipanema Beach		interesting	
boring			crowded	
exciting			fun	

> Ipanema Beach is beautiful.

UNIT 8 Teen Time

2 Language focus

What's it like?
What's it like?
It's fun.

A Tyler and Yoshi talk about their favorite places. Listen and practice.

Tyler What's your favorite place in Tokyo, Yoshi?
Yoshi It's Odaiba.
Tyler What's it like?
Yoshi It's fun. There are a lot of things there. There are beaches, parks, stores, and museums. Joypolis Park is also there.
Tyler What's it like?
Yoshi It's great. It has a lot of video games.

B Complete the conversation. Listen and check. Then practice.

Tyler I like New York a lot.
Yoshi _____
Tyler It's big and exciting. I like the Empire State Building, too.
Yoshi _____
Tyler It's really beautiful. And there's an observatory on the 102nd floor.

C Ask a classmate about a favorite place in your town or city.

A What's your favorite place in . . . . . . ?
B It's . . . .
A What's it like?
B It's . . . .

3 Listening

Jenny, Paulo, and Sandra talk to Tyler about a museum. What's it like? Listen and check (✓) the correct words.

	Beautiful	Interesting	Exciting	Fun	Crowded	Boring
Jenny	✓	☐	✓	☐	☐	☐
Paulo	☐	☐	☐	☐	☐	☐
Sandra	☐	☐	☐	☐	☐	☐

Teen Time 101

Lesson 30 Talent show

1 Vocabulary

A There is a talent show at Kent International School. Look at the bulletin board. Label the photos with the words in the box. Then listen and practice.

☐ dance ☑ play Ping-Pong ☐ sing
☐ draw ☐ play the guitar ☐ skateboard

Enter the Talent Show!

1. play Ping-Pong
2.
3.
4.
5.
6.

B Who in your class can enter the talent show? Write one name for each category.

Category	Name	Category	Name
dance		sing	
play the guitar		play Ping-Pong	
draw		skateboard	

102 Unit 8

2 Language focus

can / can't

I **can** dance.   She **can't** sing.
Can you dance? **Can** she sing?
Yes, I **can**.   **No**, she **can't**.

Use *can* for all subjects:
I, you, he, she, we, they

A Paulo and Sandra talk about the talent show. Listen and practice.

Paulo Look! There's a talent show on Sunday. Let's enter.
Sandra Um . . . no, thanks.
Paulo Oh, come on. I can play the guitar. I can't sing. Can you sing?
Sandra No, I can't. I can't sing at all.
Paulo Can you dance?
Sandra Yes, I can. But . . .
Paulo So, let's enter the show.
Sandra You and me? You're kidding! I'm too shy.

B Write two things Paulo and Sandra can and can't do. Then listen and check.

1. Paulo _____ .
2. Paulo _____ .
3. Sandra _____ .
4. Sandra _____ .

3 Speaking

Read the survey. Write questions 4 and 5. Complete the survey for yourself. Then ask a classmate the questions.

What can you do?	You		Your classmate	
	Yes	No	Yes	No
1. Can you skateboard?	☐	☐	☐	☐
2. Can you draw?	☐	☐	☐	☐
3. Can you play Ping-Pong?	☐	☐	☐	☐
4. _____	☐	☐	☐	☐
5. _____	☐	☐	☐	☐

Can you skateboard?

Yes, I can.   No, I can't.

4 Pronunciation   *can* and *can't*

A Listen to the pronunciation of *can* and *can't*.

He **can** sing.   He **can't** dance.

B Listen and check (✓) *can* or *can't*. Then listen again and practice.

1. ☐ can   2. ☐ can   3. ☐ can   4. ☐ can   5. ☐ can
   ☐ can't   ☐ can't   ☐ can't   ☐ can't   ☐ can't

Teen Time   103

Lessons 29 & 30 Mini-review

1 Language check

A Write a question and answer for each picture.

1. *Can she sing?*
   No, she can't.

2. _____

3. _____

4. _____

B Match the questions to the answers.

1. What's your home like? _b_
2. Can you swim? ____
3. What's your best friend like? ____
4. Is your English class interesting? ____
5. What's your country like? ____
6. Can your teacher play soccer? ____

a. She's fun and really friendly.
b. It's nice. It has four bedrooms.
c. Yes, I can. It's really fun!
d. Yes, it is. And my teacher is nice, too.
e. No, she can't. But she can play tennis.
f. It's beautiful. But some places are crowded.

C Now ask and answer the questions in Part B. Give your own information.

What's your home like?   It's . . . .

D What's each place like? Write sentences about the places.

- ☐ beautiful ☐ crowded ☑ fun
- ☐ boring ☐ exciting ☐ interesting

Ipanema Beach

Q: What's it like?
A: It's fun.

Paris, France

Q: What's it like?
A: _____

New York City

Q: What's it like?
A: _____

Amusement Park

Q: _____
A: _____

The Museum of Modern Art

Q: _____
A: _____

the bus stop

Q: _____
A: _____

2 Listening

Listen to the conversations. Circle the correct answers.

1. He (can / can't) sing.
2. She (can / can't) dance.
3. He (can / can't) play Ping-Pong.
4. They (can / can't) draw.
5. She (can / can't) play the guitar.
6. They (can / can't) skateboard.

Go to page 121 for the Game.

Teen Time **105**

Lesson 31 — School fashion

1 Vocabulary

A These three students want new school uniforms. Listen and write their names under the correct pictures.

☐ Mateo ☐ Min ☐ George

_____   _____   _____

B Listen and practice.

C Look at the colors. Listen and practice.

1. blue
2. white
3. green
4. pink
5. orange
6. red
7. black
8. brown
9. yellow
10. purple

D Look at Part A. Complete the descriptions of the school uniforms.

adjective + noun
white blouse
black shoes

1. Min's school uniform is a __pink__ blouse, a blue __skirt__, __black__ shoes, and a blue __sweater__.
2. George's school uniform is a _____ shirt, a green _____, a _____ tie, and _____ pants.
3. Mateo's school uniform is a _____ T-shirt, _____ shorts, yellow _____, and _____ sneakers.

106   Unit 8

2 Language focus

A Charlie and Lucas talk about their new school uniform. Listen and practice.

> **What color is / are . . . ?**
> **What color is** the shirt?
> **It's** white.
> **What color are** the pants?
> **They're** blue.

Charlie Oh, wow! There's a new school uniform for next year.
Lucas Really? What's it like?
Charlie It's OK. There's a shirt, a jacket, and pants.
Lucas What color is the shirt?
Charlie It's white.
Lucas That's nice. What color are the pants?
Charlie They're blue.
Lucas And what color is the jacket?
Charlie It's purple.
Lucas Purple? Oh, no!
Charlie Lucas, I'm kidding. The jacket is blue, too.

B What is your dream uniform like? Complete the questions with *is* or *are*. Then answer the questions. Tell your classmates.

1. What color ___is___ the shirt? _It's orange._
2. What color _____ the pants? _____
3. What color _____ the socks? _____
4. What color _____ the sweater? _____
5. What color _____ the shoes? _____

> The shirt is orange. The pants are . . .

3 Listening

Four students talk on the radio about school fashion. Listen and number the pictures.

Lesson 32 — Teen tastes

1 Vocabulary

A Read about students' favorite things. Match the photos to the correct sentences. Then listen and practice.

- ☐ My favorite music is rap.
- ☐ My favorite school subject is biology.
- ☐ *1* My favorite food is pizza.
- ☐ My favorite food is hot dogs.
- ☐ My favorite music is rock.
- ☐ My favorite music is classical.
- ☐ My favorite school subject is Italian.
- ☐ My favorite food is hamburgers.

1
2
3
4
5
6
7
8

B Complete these statements. Then tell your classmates.

My favorite music is _____.

My favorite school subject is _____.

My favorite food is _____.

> My favorite music is . . .

108 Unit 8

2 Language focus

love / like / don't like
I **love** rock music.
I **like** rap music.
I **don't like** classical music.

A What do Yoshi and Jenny like? Listen and practice.

I'm a big music fan. I love rock music, and I like rap music. I can play the electric guitar. I don't like classical music. I think it's boring. My friends and I have a rock band. It's really cool.

Yoshi

I love school! I really like all of my classes, and I like my teachers and my friends. The food in the cafeteria is great. There are hot dogs and hamburgers. There's one thing I don't like about school – the homework!

Jenny

B What about you? Complete the statements with *love*, *like*, or *don't like*. Then compare with a classmate.

1. I _____ rap music.
2. I _____ math.
3. I _____ soccer.
4. I _____ pizza.
5. I _____ English.
6. I _____ the beach.
7. I _____ the first day of school.
8. I _____ classical music.
9. I _____ hot dogs.
10. I _____ my first name.
11. I _____ my city / town.
12. I _____ my school.

I love rap music. I think it's cool.

I don't like rap music. I think it's boring.

3 Listening

Nicole talks about her favorite things. Listen and check (✓) the correct things.

Sport
☑ volleyball
☐ tennis

Music
☐ rap
☐ rock

School subject
☐ art
☐ science

Food
☐ hamburgers
☐ pizza

Clothing
☐ jacket
☐ sneakers

Get Connected
UNIT 8

A Read the article quickly. Write three things you can do at a New York City street fair.

1. _____   3. _____
2. _____

New York City Street Fairs

What are New York City street **fairs** like? Well, they're really fun. Some fairs are small **block** or neighborhood parties. But some fairs are really big – 30 city blocks long! There's great food, good music, and a lot of **shopping**.

So, is the shopping good? Yes! The shopping is awesome – and **cheap**. And there are some really nice things. You can **buy** bags, T-shirts, sneakers, CDs, toys – everything!

Are you a big music fan? At some street fairs, you can walk around and listen to music. There's rock, rap, and **jazz**, too!

And, there's a lot of good food, too – pizza, hot dogs, and ice cream. There's food from all around the world. You can eat Italian, Thai, Mexican, Chinese food, and more.

So, go to a street fair for an exciting time! It's crowded, but it's fun!

Go to page 125 for the Vocabulary Practice.

B Read the article slowly. Check your answers in Part A.

C Are these statements true or false? Write *True* or *False*. Then correct the false statements.

1. All New York City street fairs are really big.
   False.   Some New York City street fairs are small.

2. You can buy a lot of really cool things there.
   _____

3. You can't listen to music at a street fair.
   _____

4. There's only American food at street fairs.
   _____

5. A street fair is exciting, fun, and crowded.
   _____

What's it like?

A 🔊 Jessica and Ruben are talking about the school fair. Listen and answer the questions.

1. Is the school fair on Friday? _No, it's on Saturday._
2. What's the school fair like? _____
3. Can Jessica juggle? _____
4. What colors are the school colors? _____
5. Can Ruben sing? _____

B What do you think? Write *I agree* or *I disagree* (don't agree).

1. School fairs are fun. _____
2. Talent shows are exciting. _____
3. Pizza, hot dogs, and hamburgers are healthy. _____
4. Races are cool. _____

Your turn

A Answer the questions about a fair (or event) at your school, or in your neighborhood or city.

1. What's the name of the fair / event? _____
2. When is it? _____
3. Where is it? _____
4. What can you do there? _____
5. What's it like? _____

B Write about the fair or event. Use the answers in Part A to help you.

I really like the _____

Teen Time 111

Unit 8 Review

Language chart review

What's ... like?	love / like / don't like	can / can't
What's New York like? 　It's fun. **What color is / are ... ?** What color is Kate's sweater? 　It's blue. What color are Kate's shoes? 　They're black.	I love this town. I like the mall. I don't like my room.	I can sing. He can't sing. Can you sing? 　Yes, I can. / No, I can't. Can they play soccer? 　Yes, they can. / No, they can't. can't = cannot

A Amy meets Ivan. Complete the conversation with the sentences in the box. Write the letters in the boxes.

☐ a. I can play the guitar. I'm pretty good.　　☐ d. No, I can't. I don't like baseball. Can you play?
☐ b. Well, I love soccer, but there are no　　　☐ e. It's great! The people are friendly, and there
　　soccer fields near here.　　　　　　　　　　　are a lot of beautiful places.
☑ c. Yes, I am. I'm Ivan.　　　　　　　　　　　☐ f. Yeah, it's interesting. But this town is boring.

Amy Excuse me. Are you Jon's cousin from Mexico?
Ivan [c]
Amy Hi, I'm Amy. So, what's Mexico like?
Ivan [   ]
Amy Wow, that's cool! Do you like the U.S.?
Ivan [   ]
Amy Really? Why is it boring? I love our town.
Ivan [   ]
Amy Yeah, you're right. But there's a baseball field. Can you play baseball?
Ivan [   ]
Amy Yes, I can. I love baseball. So, what other things can you do?
Ivan [   ]
Amy Really? I can play the guitar, too.

B What do you think Ivan and Amy say? Circle the correct words.

Ivan
1. I (like / don't like) the U.S.
2. I (like / don't like) this town.
3. I (can / can't) play baseball.

Amy
4. I (can / can't) play baseball.
5. I (like / don't like) this town.
6. I (like / don't like) music.

C Look at the picture on page 112. What are Amy's clothes like? What are Ivan's clothes like? Circle the false sentences.

1. (Ivan's pants are brown.)
2. Amy's T-shirt is red.
3. Ivan's shirt is white.
4. Amy's skirt is blue.
5. Amy's shoes are green.
6. Ivan's sneakers are purple.
7. Amy's hat is blue.
8. Ivan's jacket is black.

D Now correct the false sentences in Part C.

1. Ivan's pants are black.
2. _____
3. _____
4. _____

E Write the questions or the answers about Andrea.

1. **Q:** What color is Andrea's blouse?
   A: It's white.
2. **Q:** What color are Andrea's pants?
   A: _____
3. **Q:** _____
   A: It's green.
4. **Q:** What color is Andrea's sweater?
   A: _____
5. **Q:** _____
   A: They're pink.
6. **Q:** What color is Andrea's hat?
   A: _____

F Write questions beginning with *Can you*. Then answer the questions with your own information.

1. (sing)   **Q:** Can you sing?
                   A: _____
2. (skateboard)   **Q:** _____
                   A: _____
3. (draw people)   **Q:** _____
                   A: _____
4. (play tennis)   **Q:** _____
                   A: _____

Go to page 133 for the Theme Project.

Game Connect it!

A Connect the words in the maze to make five sentences.

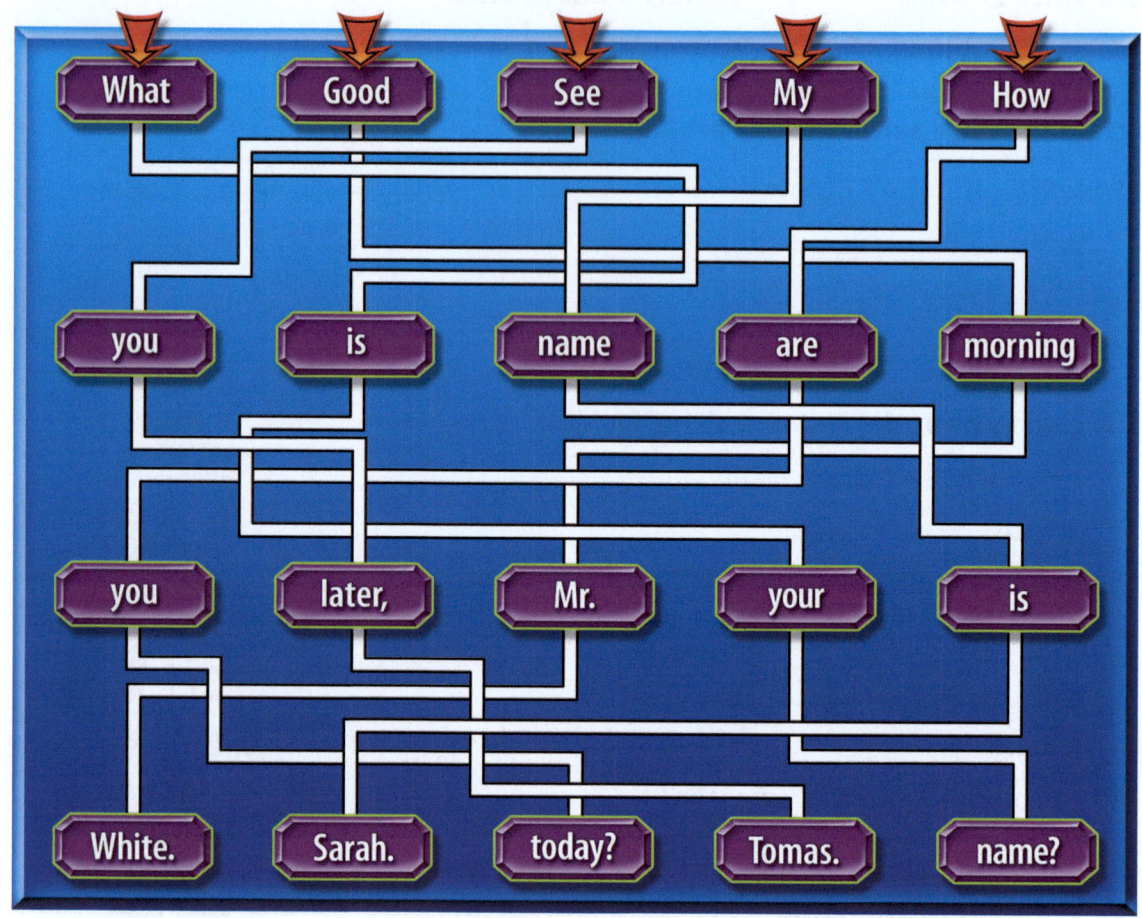

B Complete the conversations with four sentences from Part A.

1. **A** _____
   B Hello, Todd.
2. **A** _____
   B Fine, thanks.
3. **A** _____
   B Bye-bye.
4. **A** _____
   B My name is Sarah.

C Now practice with a classmate. Use your own information.

What's your name?   My name is ....

Unit 2 Game Crossword puzzle

Look at the pictures to complete the crossword.

Across

2. Mr. Armstrong is a great _____.
6. Josh is my _____.
7. Mike isn't a tennis player. He's a _____.
8. Tasha Reed is my favorite _____.

Down

1. Mr. Brooks isn't a science teacher. He's a _____.
3. Margie Frick is in good movies. She's my favorite _____.
4. My favorite song is *In the World*. The _____ is Daniela Ella.
5. Jackie is my _____. She's my science partner, too.

Game What's this?

A What are these objects? Guess. Label each photo.

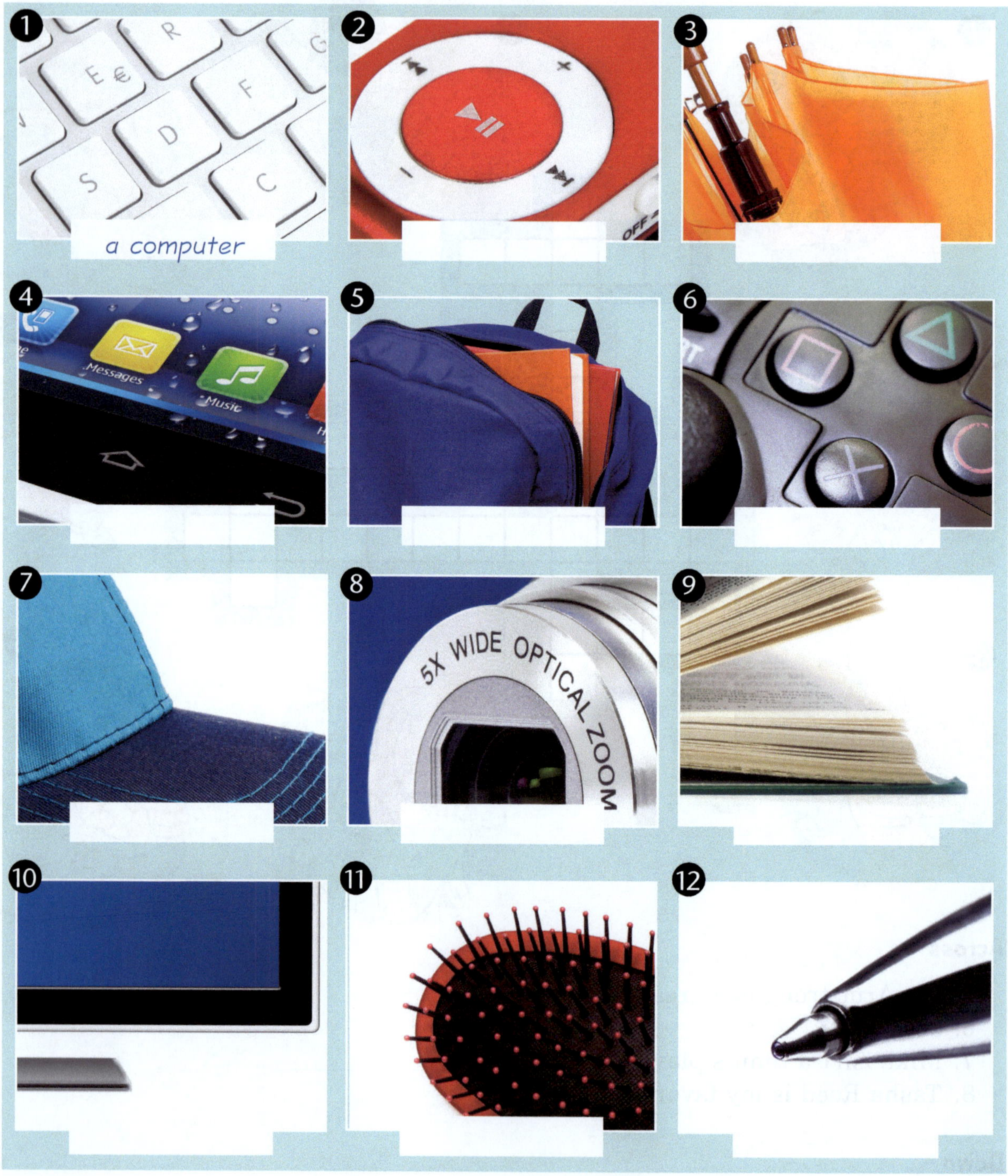

1. a computer
2.
3.
4.
5.
6.
7.
8.
9.
10.
11.
12.

B How many of your answers are correct? Compare with a classmate.

You What's this?
Classmate I think it's a computer.
You I think it's a television.

Unit 4 Game — Find the differences

How is Picture 2 different from Picture 1? Complete the chart.

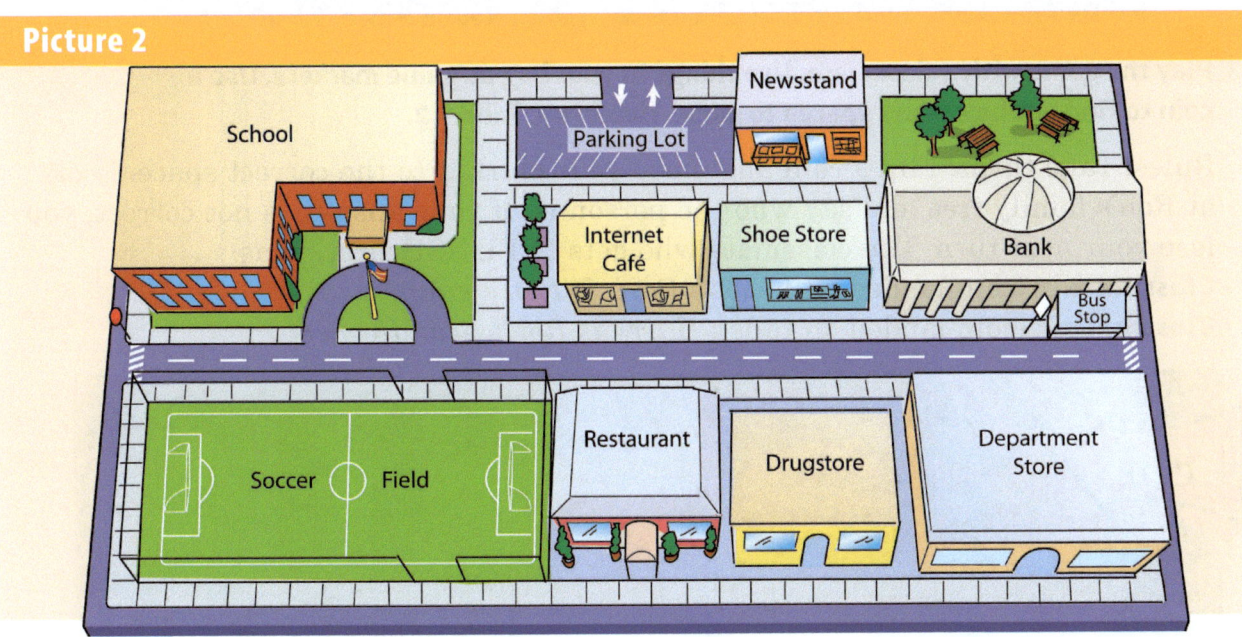

Picture 1	Picture 2
The bus stop is in front of the school.	The bus stop is in front of the bank.
The school is across from the park.	
The parking lot is behind the bank.	
The newsstand is in front of the shoe store.	
The drugstore is between the movie theater and the department store.	

Game Who's this?

A Look at Ron's family tree. Who are the people in his family?

B Play the game with a classmate. Use things in your bag as game markers. Use a coin to find out how many spaces to move. Heads = 1, Tails = 2.

Rules: Take turns. Flip a coin and move your marker to the correct space. Look at Ron's family tree and say who the person is. If your answer is not correct, you lose your next turn. The classmate who gets to FINISH first, wins.
Classmate 1 (coin landed on heads): *Barb is Ron's mother.*
Classmate 2 (coin landed on tails): *Harry is Ron's grandfather.*

Unit 6 Game Do you remember?

Look at the picture for one minute. Close your book.
Your teacher asks questions. What do you remember?

Teacher Are there any tables?
Team A Yes, there are.

Teacher Is there a tennis court?
Team B No, there isn't.

Unit 7 — Game Countries puzzle

A Write the missing letters to make country names.

A <u>u s t r a l i</u> a
B _ _ _ _ _ _ l
C _ _ _ _ _ a
E _ _ _ _ _ _ d
F _ _ _ _ _ e
I _ _ _ _ a
M _ _ _ _ _ o
S _ _ _ _ n

B Write the country names from Part A to complete the puzzle.

Unit 8 Game Can you...?

Play the game with a classmate. Use things in your bag as game markers.
Use a coin to find out how many spaces to move. Heads = 1, Tails = 2.

Rules:
- Take turns. Flip a coin and move to the correct space.
- Read the question. Can you do what it says?
  ▶ Yes. Follow the green arrow and move ahead.
  ◀ No. Follow the purple arrow and move back.
- On a "free space," ask a classmate any question. Keep your marker on that space until your next turn.
- The person who gets to FINISH first, wins.

START

Can you name six months of the year?
2 SPACES →
← 1 SPACE

Can you answer this question? *What time is it now?*
3 SPACES →
← GO BACK TO START.

Take Another Turn!

Can you complete this sentence? *My birthday is on _____.*
1 SPACE →
← 1 SPACE

Can you name five school subjects?
← 3 SPACES
← 4 SPACES

Free Space! Ask a classmate a question.

Can you say *hello* in three languages?
1 SPACE →
← 4 SPACES

Can you name five rooms in a house?
2 SPACES →
← 1 SPACE

Free Space! Ask a classmate a question.

Can you spell your partner's first and last names?
2 SPACES →
← 2 SPACES

Can you say one thing you can do and one thing you can't do?
1 SPACE →
← GO BACK TO START.

Take Another Turn!

Can you complete this sentence? *Mother's Day is in _____.*
3 SPACES →
← 1 SPACE

Can you say the days of the week?
2 SPACES →
← GO BACK TO START.

FINISH

Can you answer this question? *What's your best friend like?*
1 SPACE →
← GO BACK TO START.

Can you count to 50 in one minute?
2 SPACES →
← 5 SPACES

Free Space! Ask a classmate a question.

Can you name five nationalities?
1 SPACE →
← 3 SPACES

Get Connected Vocabulary Practice

Unit 1

Complete the sentences with the words in the box.

☐ candy bar (n.)   ☑ dog (n.)   ☐ like (v.)   ☐ music (n.)   ☐ sushi (n.)

1. This is my ___dog___ , Max.

2. I _____ school.

3. That _____ is great.

4. I like _____ .

5. This is a great _____ .

Unit 2

Complete the sentences with the words in the box.

☐ funny (adj.)   ☐ pineapple (n.)   ☐ show (n.)   ☑ sport (n.)

1. My favorite ___sport___ is tennis.
2. That cartoon is so _____ .
3. My favorite _____ is on TV now.
4. This _____ is from Brazil. It's so good!

Unit 3

Complete the sentences with the words in the box.

☐ cat (n.) ☐ spider (n.) ☐ tree house (n.)
☐ smiles (v.) ☑ teenager (n.) ☐ virtual (adj.)

1. Marc is 13. He's a _teenager_ .
2. It's not a dog – it's a _____ .
3. He has posters, a chair, and books in his _____ .
4. My friend's pet is weird. It's a _____ .
5. Look at this _____ room on my Web site. It's cool.
6. She _____ a lot. She's very happy.

Unit 4

Match the sentences to the correct pictures.

1. That bookstore is the <u>biggest (adj.)</u> one. _c_

    a.

2. <u>Paintball (n.)</u> is really cool. ____

    b.

3. <u>Waterslides (n.)</u> are fun. ____

    c.

4. A <u>jungle (n.)</u> is interesting. ____

    d.

5. Let's go to the <u>amusement park (n.)</u>. ____

    e.

Get Connected Vocabulary Practice

Unit 5

Complete the sentences with the words in the box.

☐ different (adj.) ☐ lucky (adj.) ☐ run (v.)
☐ homeschooled (adj.) ☐ oldest (adj.) ☑ youngest (adj.)

1. My little sister is the __youngest__ child in my family.
2. I don't live with my grandparents. They live in a _____ city.
3. Let's _____ in the park together.
4. My friends and family are great! I'm so _____ .
5. His mother is his teacher and his school is at home. He's _____ .
6. My _____ cousin is 25. My youngest cousin is 5.

Unit 6

The underlined words belong in other sentences. Write the words where they belong.

1. Summer (n.) with tennis balls is really fun. __Juggling__
2. That famous model studies summer camp (n.). _____
3. There are juggling (n.) classes in the computer lab. _____
4. The 3D animation (n.) classes are in the school kitchen. _____
5. Fashion design (n.) is really cool. There are volleyball games, contests, art classes, talent shows, picnics, and more! _____
6. In cooking (n.), people go to the beach a lot. _____

Unit 7

Complete the sentences with the words in the box.

☐ celebrations (n.)   ☑ receive (v.)   ☐ windows (n.)
☐ important (adj.)   ☐ throw (v.)

1. People __receive__ a lot of cards and candy on Valentine's Day.
2. Thanksgiving is a very _____ holiday in America.
3. There are two big _____ in my bedroom.
4. On July 4th, there are many _____ in the U.S.
5. Kids think it is fun to _____ water at each other at the beach.

Unit 8

Complete the advertisement with the words in the box.

☐ blocks (n.)   ☐ cheap (adj.)   ☐ jazz (n.)
☐ buy (v.)   ☑ Fair (n.)   ☐ shopping (v.)

Come to the City Park __Fair__ this Saturday, May 5th! It's five city _____ long! The _____ is great – there are T-shirts, CDs, posters, and other things. You can listen to rock and _____ , too. _____ your favorite foods – they're _____ , but good. See you Saturday from 11:00 a.m. to 4:00 p.m. for a fun day at the fair!

Get Connected Vocabulary Practice

Theme Project: Make a personal information poster.
Theme: Relationships
Goal: To create stronger relationships in your classroom community

At Home

Read about Andréia.

My first name is Andréia. My last name is Lima. My nickname is Déia. My e-mail address is andreialima789@school.dt.br. My favorite subject is science.

Complete the sentence. Use your dictionary, if necessary.

My favorite school subject is _____ .

Draw a picture or bring a photo of yourself to class.

In Class

Make a poster. Ask each other *What's your . . . ?* Write the answers. Use the sample poster as a model.

Choose a group leader. Present your poster to another group.

"This is Megumi."

"Hi, Megumi."

"Hello. This is my picture. My last name is Ohno. My nickname is Meg. My e-mail address is megumio@school.net. My favorite subject is math."

Display the posters in your classroom. Walk around and look at all of them. Who has an interesting nickname?

Photo				
First name	Megumi	Andrew	Maria	Luciano de
Last name	Ohno	Smith	Valdez	Almeida
Nickname	Meg	Andy	Mari	Lú
E-mail address	megumio@school.net	andysmith@school.net	mari@school.net	lucianolu@school.net
Favorite subject	math	English	social studies	science

Sample poster

Theme Project: Make a poster about two people who work at your school.
Theme: Citizenship
Goal: To become better acquainted with people in your school community

At Home

Read about Mr. Alvarez.

This is Mr. Alvarez. His first name is Pedro. He's a math teacher at my school. He's from Juarez. His favorite tennis player is Rafael Nadal.

Mr. Alvarez

Before Class

Talk to a worker at your school. Complete the chart. Use your dictionary, if necessary.

First name	Last name	Hometown	Job	Favorite

Draw a picture or bring a photo of the worker to class.

In Class

Look at all the people. Choose the two most interesting people.

Make a poster. Use the sample poster as a model.

Choose a group leader. Present your poster to another group.

This is Mr. Ramirez. His first name is Pablo. He's a soccer coach. He's from Guadalajara. His favorite soccer player is Nery Castillo.

This is Ms. Lopez. Her first name is . . .

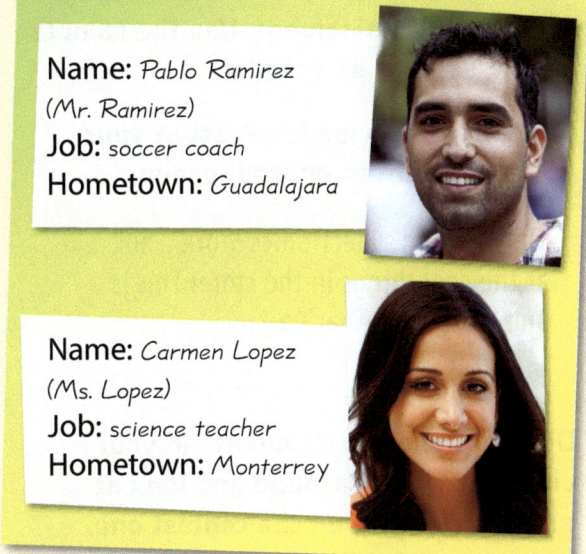

Name: *Pablo Ramirez*
(*Mr. Ramirez*)
Job: *soccer coach*
Hometown: *Guadalajara*

Name: *Carmen Lopez*
(*Ms. Lopez*)
Job: *science teacher*
Hometown: *Monterrey*

Sample poster

Display the posters in your classroom. Walk around and look at all of them. How many people do you know?

Unit 2 Theme Project

Unit 3

Theme Project: Make an advertisement for an electronics store.
Theme: Consumer awareness
Goal: To become aware of the powerful influence of advertising

At Home

Read about Paulo's favorite electronic things.

Look at my favorite electronic things. This is my laptop. It's new. This is my MP3 player. It's a radio, too. And this is my cell phone. Look! It's a camera, too. It's really cool.

Think of three electronic things. Write the names of the things. Use your dictionary, if necessary.

1. _____ 2. _____ 3. _____

Find advertisements for the three electronic things you wrote. Look in newspapers and magazines. Bring the advertisements to class.

In Class

- Look at all the advertisements. Choose five things. Choose the coolest advertisements for them.

- Choose a name for your electronics store. Make an advertisement. Use the sample advertisement as a model.

- Choose a group leader. Present your advertisement to another group.

  > This is Steph's Electronics Store. Look at the cool things in the store! This is an MP3 player. That's a . . .

- Display the advertisements in your classroom. Walk around and look at all of them. Vote on the coolest one.

Sample store advertisement

128 Unit 3 Theme Project

Theme Project: Make a guide for visitors to your city.
Theme: Citizenship
Goal: To learn more about your city or town; to provide useful information for visitors

At Home

Read about John's hometown and his suggestions for visitors.

Welcome to my city – Chicago! Go to the John Hancock Tower. It's on Michigan Avenue. It's really tall. Go to the top – it's a great view. Water Tower Place is also on Michigan Avenue. It's a big mall. Have a sandwich there and do some shopping. My favorite bookstore is across from Water Tower Place. Read a magazine there and have a soda there. Let's go together sometime!

John Hancock Tower   Water Tower Place

What places in your city or town should a visitor know about? Complete the chart. Use your dictionary, if necessary.

Place: _____   Place: _____

Location: _____   Location: _____

Suggestion: _____   Suggestion: _____

Draw pictures or bring photos of the places to class.

In Class

- Look at all the places. Choose two places.

- Make a page for a guide on a piece of paper. Use the sample page as a model.

- Choose a group leader. Present your places to another group.

    Go to Pike Place Market. It's on Pike Street. Have a sandwich and a soda there.

- Give your group's page to the teacher. The teacher staples together the pages. Pass around the guide. What is your favorite place? Why?

Pike Place Market
Pike Street
Have a sandwich and a soda!

Space Needle
Seattle Center
Go to the top!

Sample guide page

Unit 4 Theme Project   **129**

Theme Project: Make a group photo album.
Themes: Relationships; multiculturalism
Goal: To create stronger relationships in your classroom community

At Home

Read about Tomoko's favorite relative.

My name is Tomoko Fuji. I have a lot of nice relatives. My favorite relative is my uncle. His name is Hiro. He's my mother's brother. He's 46. He's smart and really funny. I think he's handsome, too!

Hiro

Complete the chart about your favorite relative. Use your dictionary, if necessary.

Name	Age	Relationship	What's he / she like?

Draw a picture or bring a photo of your favorite relative to class.

In Class

1. Make a photo album page of your relative. Use the sample album page as a model.

2. Tell your group about your relative.

   > This is my cousin, Sofia. She's 21. She's tall and thin. She's really friendly. Sofia is my favorite relative.

3. Make a group photo album. Make a cover for your photo album. Then staple together all of your pages and the cover to make your album.

4. Choose a group leader. Present your photo album to another group.

5. Display the photo albums in your classroom. Walk around and look at all of them. Which person do you want to meet? Why?

Sofia
Cousin, 21

Sample photo album page

130 Unit 5 Theme Project

Theme Project: Make a poster of a dream school ("cool school").
Theme: Citizenship
Goal: To learn to present an idea for an ideal school

At Home

Read about Kevin's ideas for his "cool school."

My cool school is great! There's an auditorium in the school. We have juggling class there. There's a football field in the school. We have marching band there. There's a computer lab in the school. We have Web design class there. I love my school!

Think of your "cool school." What facilities does it have? What classes does it have? Complete the chart. Use your dictionary, if necessary.

Facility	Class
1.	
2.	
3.	

Draw pictures or bring photos of the facilities to class.

In Class

- Choose three subjects for classes at your "cool school." Choose a facility to have each subject.

- Make a poster. Use the sample poster as a model.

- Choose a group leader. Present your poster to another group.

> This is our "cool school." There is a media center in our school. We have film-making class there . . .

- Display the posters in your classroom. Walk around and look at all of them. Vote on the best "cool school."

Sample poster

Unit 6 Theme Project   131

Unit 7

Theme Project: Make an informational booklet about different countries.
Theme: Cultural diversity
Goal: To learn about different countries and cultures

At Home

Read about Kenya.

- Kenya is in Africa. There are mountains in Kenya. Mt. Kenya is a very famous mountain. There are lions, elephants, and other wild animals in Kenya.
- Kenyan people speak English and Swahili.
- Jamhuri is Kenyan Independence Day. It is on December 12th. There are parades and fireworks.
- Mercy Myra is a famous Kenyan. She's a singer.

Mount Kenya

Choose a country. Complete the chart. Use your dictionary, if necessary.

Country: _____
Continent: _____
Language: _____

Important day: _____
Famous person: _____
Other: _____

Draw pictures or bring photos of the country you chose to class.

In Class

1. **Make a page for the country you chose. Use the sample page as a model.**

2. **Tell your group about your country.**

   > South Korea is in Asia. Korean people speak Korean . . .

3. **Make a group booklet. Make a cover for your booklet. Then staple together all of your pages and the cover to make your booklet.**

4. **Choose a group leader. Present your booklet to another group.**

5. **Display the booklets in your classroom. Walk around and look at all of them. Vote on the most interesting booklet.**

South Korea is in Asia. Korean people speak Korean. Students study Korean and English, too. Korean New Year is a big holiday. It starts on a different day every year. It is usually in February. BoA is a famous Korean. She is a singer.

Sample informational booklet page

Theme Project: Make a pair of bookmarks of healthy foods and activities.
Theme: Health and fitness
Goal: To become more aware of healthy foods and activities

At Home

Read about the health tips.

It's great to be healthy. So, eat healthy foods and do healthy activities. Potato chips and candy aren't healthy snacks. Choose healthy ones – eat an apple or a carrot.

Choose healthy activities, too. Ride your bike to school or play basketball on the weekend. Be active – it's good for you!

Write three healthy foods and three healthy activities. Use your dictionary, if necessary.

Healthy foods	Healthy activities
1.	1.
2.	2.
3.	3.

In Class

- Look at all the lists.
- Choose one food and one activity you like. Make two bookmarks. Use the sample bookmarks as models.
- Present your bookmarks to your group.

> Eat bananas. They're healthy.
> Walk to school. It's good for you!

- Display all the bookmarks in your classroom. Walk around and look at all of them. What are your favorite healthy foods and activities?

Sample bookmarks

Unit 8 Theme Project

Word List

This list includes the key words and phrases in *Connect Second Edition* Student's Book 1. The numbers next to each word are the page numbers on which the words first appear.

Key Vocabulary

Aa
a (19) ___
about (5) ___
across from (46) ___
actor (18) ___
address book (30) ___
after (8) ___
after [for time] (80) ___
afternoon (4) ___
age (22) ___
alarm clock (32) ___
all (87) ___
alphabet [a–z] (10) ___
already (81) ___
also (33) ___
always (95) ___
am (2) ___
American (88) ___
amusement park (54) ___
an (32) ___
and (17) ___
animals (100) ___
any (52) ___
apartment (64) ___
April (92) ___
are (5) ___
around (28) ___
art (78) ___
at (28) ___
at all (103) ___
athletic field (74) ___
auditorium (74) ___
August (92) ___
aunt (58) ___
Australia (25) ___
Australia Day (93) ___
Australian (88) ___
avenue (46) ___

Bb
back (2) ___
backpack (30) ___
bad (5) ___
bag (30) ___
band concert (80) ___
bank (46) ___
baseball (74) ___
basketball (16) ___
bathroom (66) ___
beach (52) ___

beautiful (84) ___
bed (38) ___
bedroom (66) ___
behind (46) ___
Belize (86) ___
best friend (16) ___
between (46) ___
bicycle (36) ___
big (64) ___
biggest (54) ___
biology (108) ___
birthday (22) ___
black (106) ___
block (110) ___
blouse (106) ___
blue (106) ___
board (72) ___
book (30) ___
bookcase (72) ___
bookstore (50) ___
bored (52) ___
boring (84) ___
bowling alley (50) ___
boy (87) ___
Brazil (24) ___
Brazilian (88) ___
British (88) ___
brother (37) ___
brown (106) ___
brush (30) ___
burger (76) ___
bus stop (44) ___
but (31) ___
buy (110) ___
bye (9) ___
bye-bye (9) ___

Cc
cabinet (72) ___
café (28) ___
cafeteria (74) ___
calculator (32) ___
camera (30) ___
can (28) ___
Canada (25) ___
Canadian (88) ___
candy bar (12) ___
candy store (50) ___
can't (102) ___
card (11) ___

Carnaval (93) ___
cartoon character (18) ___
cat (40) ___
CD / DVD player (72) ___
celebration (96) ___
cell phone (32) ___
chair (38) ___
cheap (110) ___
child (59) ___
children (59) ___
Children's Day (93) ___
Chinese (76) ___
city (64) ___
class (20) ___
classical (music) (108) ___
classmate (2) ___
classroom (64) ___
coach (16) ___
Colombia (24) ___
Colombian (89) ___
color (107) ___
come (84) ___
comic book (36) ___
computer lab (74) ___
computer partner (16) ___
cooking (82) ___
cool (32) ___
country (67) ___
cousin (58) ___
crazy (60) ___
crowded (100) ___
cute (19) ___

Dd
Dad (17) ___
dance [verb] (102) ___
day (79) ___
dear (73) ___
December (92) ___
department store (46) ___
desk (38) ___
desktop computer (32) ___
different (68) ___
difficult (78) ___
dining room (66) ___
do (11) ___
dog (12) ___
don't like (108) ___
downtown (46) ___
draw (102) ___

dream (home) (67) _____
dresser (38) _____
drugstore (46) _____

Ee
easy (78) _____
eight (22) _____
eighteen (22) _____
eighteenth (94) _____
eighth (94) _____
eighty (58) _____
electric (guitar) (109) _____
eleven (22) _____
eleventh (94) _____
e-mail (84) _____
England (86) _____
English (65) _____
enter (102) _____
e-pal (24) _____
eraser (30) _____
evening (4) _____
every (79) _____
everybody (51) _____
everyday (30) _____
excited (81) _____
exciting (100) _____

Ff
facility (74) _____
fair (110) _____
family (58) _____
famous (84) _____
fan (19) _____
fashion design (82) _____
fashion show (80) _____
father (58) _____
Father's Day (92) _____
favorite (16) _____
February (92) _____
fifteen (22) _____
fifteenth (94) _____
fifth (94) _____
fifty (58) _____
fine (5) _____
fine arts (84) _____
first (11) _____
five (22) _____
floor (101) _____
food (76) _____
football (74) _____
for (5) _____
forty (58) _____
four (22) _____
fourteen (22) _____
fourteenth (94) _____
fourth (94) _____
France (88) _____
French (88) _____
Friday (79) _____
friend (16) _____
friendly (60) _____
from (24) _____
fun (76) _____
funny (26) _____

Gg
game (80) _____
garage (66) _____
geography (28) _____
girl (87) _____
global (28) _____
go (8) _____
goal (48) _____
good (4) _____
good-bye (9) _____
grandfather (58) _____
grandmother (58) _____
grandparents (58) _____
great (5) _____
green (106) _____
guitar (102) _____
gym (74) _____

Hh
half (past) (80) _____
hamburger (76) _____
handsome (60) _____
happy (64) _____
happy birthday (23) _____
has (59) _____
hat (30) _____
have (59) _____
have (a soda) (52) _____
he (19) _____
health (78) _____
hello (2) _____
her (17) _____
here (11) _____
hey (33) _____
hi (2) _____
him (37) _____
his (17) _____
history (78) _____
holiday (92) _____
home (45) _____
homeschooled (68) _____
homework (109) _____
hot (52) _____
hot dog (108) _____
house (67) _____
how (5) _____
hungry (47) _____
hurry (45) _____

Ii
I (2) _____
idea (53) _____
important (96) _____
in (38) _____
Independence Day (92) _____
India (86) _____
in front of (46) _____
inside (64) _____
interesting (84) _____
international (49) _____
Internet (33) _____
Internet café (44) _____
introduce (87) _____
is (2) _____
it (28) _____
Italian (108) _____

Jj
jacket (106) _____
January (92) _____
Japan (25) _____
Japanese (88) _____
jazz (110) _____
juggling (82) _____
July (92) _____
June (92) _____
jungle (54) _____
just (25) _____

Kk
kangaroo (100) _____
keypad (33) _____
kidding (25) _____
kitchen (66) _____
know (25) _____

Ll
language lab (74) _____
laptop (32) _____
last (11) _____
late (4) _____
later (9) _____
let's (8) _____
letter (65) _____
library (11) _____
like (me) (58) _____
like [verb] (12) _____
like [What's he like?] (61) _____
little (23) _____
little [a little] (61) _____
live [verb] (65) _____
living room (66) _____
look (17) _____
lost (47) _____
lot [a lot] (64) _____
love [verb] (84) _____
lucky (68) _____
lunch (79) _____

Mm
mall (50) _____
many (84) _____
map (47) _____
March (92) _____
math (16) _____
May (92) _____
me (53) _____
media center (72) _____
meet (3) _____
mess [noun] (30) _____

Mexican (88) _____
Mexico (24) _____
middle school (73) _____
minute (28) _____
Miss (4) _____
miss [verb] (64) _____
model (18) _____
Mom (31) _____
Monday (79) _____
money (53) _____
month (95) _____
more (72) _____
morning (4) _____
mother (58) _____
Mother's Day (92) _____
mountain (84) _____
movie (21) _____
movie theater (44) _____
MP3 player (32) _____
Mr. (4) _____
Mrs. (4) _____
Ms. (4) _____
museum (84) _____
music (12) _____
music store (50) _____
my (2) _____

Nn
name (2) _____
national (84) _____
nationality (88) _____
near (45) _____
neighbor (65) _____
neighborhood (64) _____
new (5) _____
newsstand (44) _____
New Year's Eve (92) _____
New Zealand (86) _____
next to (38) _____
next (year) (107) _____
nice (3) _____
night (9) _____
nine (22) _____
nineteen (22) _____
nineteenth (94) _____
ninety (58) _____
ninth (94) _____
no (22) _____
noisy (64) _____
noon (80) _____
not (5) _____
notebook (30) _____
November (92) _____
now (37) _____
number (65) _____

Oo
observatory (101) _____
o'clock (79) _____
October (92) _____
of (25) _____
OK (5) _____

old [adjective] (64) _____
old [age] (23) _____
oldest (68) _____
on (33) _____
one (22) _____
one hundred (58) _____
online (93) _____
only (23) _____
only (child) (59) _____
orange [color] (106) _____
other (75) _____
our (65) _____

Pp
paintball (54) _____
pants (106) _____
parents (58) _____
park (46) _____
parking lot (46) _____
partner (16) _____
party (95) _____
P.E. (78) _____
pen (30) _____
pencil (38) _____
pencil case (30) _____
people (16) _____
Peru (25) _____
Peruvian (88) _____
photo (25) _____
physical education (78) _____
picnic (80) _____
picture (70) _____
pineapple (26) _____
Ping-Pong (102) _____
pink (106) _____
pizza (108) _____
place (76) _____
play (52) _____
please (45) _____
popular (88) _____
Portugal (25) _____
poster (36) _____
pretty (60) _____
printer (72) _____
problem (73) _____
Puerto Rican (88) _____
Puerto Rico (88) _____
purple (106) _____

Qq
quarter (after / to) (80) _____
quiet (64) _____
quiz (88) _____

Rr
race (80) _____
radio (107) _____
rap (music) (108) _____
ready (5) _____
really [adverb] (23) _____
really [exclamation] (20) _____
receive (96) _____

red (106) _____
remote control (72) _____
restaurant (44) _____
reunion (60) _____
right (19) _____
right [correct] (11) _____
right now (93) _____
rock band (109) _____
rock (music) (108) _____
run (68) _____

Ss
sad (64) _____
same (37) _____
sandwich (52) _____
Saturday (94) _____
scanner (72) _____
schedule (79) _____
school (2) _____
science (16) _____
screen (72) _____
second (94) _____
see (9) _____
September (92) _____
serious (89) _____
seven (22) _____
seventeen (22) _____
seventeenth (94) _____
seventh (94) _____
seventy (58) _____
she (19) _____
shirt (106) _____
shoes (106) _____
shoe store (44) _____
shopping (110) _____
short (60) _____
shorts (106) _____
shy (60) _____
sing (102) _____
Singapore (86) _____
singer (18) _____
sister (23) _____
sit (down) (52) _____
six (22) _____
sixteen (22) _____
sixteenth (94) _____
sixth (94) _____
sixty (58) _____
skateboard (102) _____
skating rink (50) _____
skirt (106) _____
small (37) _____
smart (60) _____
smile (40) _____
sneakers (106) _____
so [conjunction] (19) _____
so [very] (23) _____
soccer field (48) _____
soccer player (19) _____
socks (106) _____
soda (52) _____
some (89) _____

sometimes (64) _____
soon (4) _____
sorry (49) _____
South Africa (86) _____
South Korea (88) _____
South Korean (88) _____
Spain (88) _____
Spanish [language] (78) _____
Spanish [nationality] (88) _____
speak (87) _____
spell (11) _____
spelling contest (80) _____
spider (40) _____
sports (26) _____
sports facilities (74) _____
Spring Day (80) _____
star [famous person] (18) _____
still (45) _____
street (46) _____
subject (78) _____
subway station (46) _____
suggestion (52) _____
summer (82) _____
summer camp (82) _____
Sunday (94) _____
sushi (12) _____
sweater (106) _____
swimming (52) _____
swimming pool (74) _____

Tt
talent show (102) _____
tall (60) _____
taste (108) _____
teacher (16) _____
team (48) _____
teen (100) _____
teenager (40) _____
television (32) _____
tell (37) _____
ten (22) _____
tennis court (74) _____
tennis player (18) _____
tenth (94) _____
thanks (5) _____
Thanksgiving (92) _____
thank you (5) _____
that (11) _____
the (5) _____
their (65) _____
them (57) _____
there (51) _____
these (37) _____
they (37) _____
thin (60) _____
things (30) _____
think (19) _____
third (94) _____
thirsty (52) _____
thirteen (22) _____
thirteenth (94) _____

thirtieth (94) _____
thirty (58) _____
thirty-first (94) _____
this (8) _____
those (37) _____
three (22) _____
3D animation (82) _____
throw water (96) _____
Thursday (79) _____
tie [clothing] (106) _____
time (79) _____
time [saying the time] (79) _____
tired (52) _____
to (2) _____
today (5) _____
together (53) _____
tomorrow (9) _____
too (3) _____
town (44) _____
trading card (36) _____
travel (28) _____
tree house (40) _____
T-shirt (36) _____
Tuesday (79) _____
TV (32) _____
TV show (26) _____
TV star (18) _____
twelfth (94) _____
twelve (22) _____
twentieth (94) _____
twenty (22) _____
twenty-eight (58) _____
twenty-eighth (94) _____
twenty-fifth (94) _____
twenty-first (94) _____
twenty-five (58) _____
twenty-four (58) _____
twenty-fourth (94) _____
twenty-nine (58) _____
twenty-ninth (94) _____
twenty-one (58) _____
twenty-second (94) _____
twenty-seven (58) _____
twenty-seventh (94) _____
twenty-six (58) _____
twenty-sixth (94) _____
twenty-third (94) _____
twenty-three (58) _____
twenty-two (58) _____
two (22) _____

Uu
umbrella (30) _____
uncle (58) _____
under (38) _____
uniform (107) _____
United States [the U.S.] (24) _____
used (76) _____
usually (89) _____

Vv
vacation (100) _____
Valentine's Day (92) _____
Venezuela (25) _____
very (37) _____
video arcade (50) _____
video game (32) _____
virtual (40) _____
visit (84) _____
volleyball (52) _____

Ww
wait (73) _____
wall (38) _____
wastebasket (38) _____
watch [noun] (36) _____
waterslide (54) _____
wax (100) _____
we (65) _____
Wednesday (79) _____
weird (33) _____
well (45) _____
what (3) _____
when (93) _____
where (25) _____
white (106) _____
who (17) _____
window (96) _____
wireless (33) _____
with (45) _____
world (28) _____
wow (33) _____
write (65) _____
wrong (53) _____

Yy
yard (66) _____
yeah (53) _____
year (5) _____
yellow (106) _____
yes (5) _____
you (3) _____
youngest (68) _____
your (3) _____

Zz
zero (22) _____
zoo (100) _____

Acknowledgments

Connect, Second Edition has benefited from extensive development research. The authors and publishers would like to extend their particular thanks to all the CUP editorial, production, and marketing staff, as well as the following reviewers and consultants for their valuable insights and suggestions:

Focus Groups

São Paulo **Suzi T. Almeida**, Colégio Rio Branco; **Andreia C. Alves**, Colégio Guilherme de Almeida; **Patricia Del Valle**, Colégio I. L. Peretz; **Elaine Elia**, Centro de Educação Caminho Aberto; **Rosemilda L. Falletti**, Colégio Pio XII; **Amy Foot Gomes**, Instituto D. Placidina; **Lilian I. Leventhal**, Colégio I. L. Peretz; **Adriana Pellegrino**, Colégio Santo Agostinho; **Maria de Fátima Sanchez**, Colégio Salesiano Sta. Teresinha; **Regina C. B. Saponara**, Colégio N. S. do Sion; **Neuza C. Senna**, Colégio Henri Wallon; **Camila Toniolo Silva**, Colégio I. L. Peretz; **Izaura Valverde**, Nova Escola.

Curitiba **Liana Andrade**, Colégio Medianeira; **Bianca S. Borges**, Colégio Bom Jesus; **Rosana Fernandes**, Colégio Bom Jesus; **Cecilia Honorio**, Colégio Medianeira; **Regina Linzmayer**, Colégio Bom Jesus; **Maria Cecília Piccoli**, Colégio N. S. Sion; **Ana L. Z. Pinto**, Colégio Bom Jesus; **Mary C. M. dos Santos**, Colégio Bom Jesus; **Andrea S. M. Souza**, Colégio Bom Jesus; **Juçara M. S. Tadra**, Colégio Bom Jesus.

Rio de Janeiro **Alcyrema R. Castro**, Colégio N. S. da Assunção; **Renata Frazão**, Colégio Verbo Divino; **Claudia G. Goretti**, Colégio dos Jesuítas; **Letícia Leite**, Colégio Verbo Divino; **Livia Mercuri**, WSA Idiomas; **Marta Moraes**, Colégio São Vicente de Paulo; **Claudia C. Rosa**, Colégio Santa Mônica.

Belo Horizonte **Júnia Barcelos**, Colégio Santo Agostinho; **Rachel Farias**, Colégio Edna Roriz; **Renato Galil**, Colégio Santo Agostinho; **Katia R. P. A. Lima**, Colégio Santa Maria; **Gleides A. Nonato**, Colégio Arnaldo; **Luciana Queiros**, Instituto Itapoã; **Flávia Samarane**, Colégio Logosófico González Pecotche; **Adriana Zardini**, UFMG.

Brasília **José Eugenio F. Alvim**, CIL – 01; **Rosemberg Andrade**, Colégio Presbiteriano Mackenzie; **Euzenira Araújo**, CIL – Gama; **Michelle Câmara**, CIL – Gama; **Kátia Falcomer**, Casa Thomas Jefferson; **Almerinda B. Garibaldi**, CIL – Taguatinga; **Michelle Gheller**, CIL – Taguatinga; **Anabel Cervo Lima**, CIL – Brasília; **Ana Lúcia F. de Morais**, CIL – Brazilândia; **Antonio José O. Neto**, CIL – Ceilândia; **Maria da Graça Nóbile**, Colégio Presbiteriano Mackenzie; **Denise A. Nunes**, CIL – Gama; **Suzana Oliveira**, CIL – Taguatinga; **Andréa Pacheco**, Colégio Marista João Paulo II; **Simone Peixoto**, CIL – Brasilândia; **Érica S. Rodrigues**, Colégio Presbiteriano Mackenzie; **Isaura Rodrigues**, CIL – Ceilândia; **Camila Salmazo**, Colégio Marista João Paulo II; **Maria da Guia Santos**, CIL – Gama; **Dóris Scolmeister**, CIL – Gama; **Rejane M. C. de Souza**, Colégio Santa Rosa; **Isabel Teixeira**, CIL – Taguatinga; **Marina Vazquez**, CIL – Gama.

Questionnaires

Brazil **Maria Heloísa Alves Audino**, Colégio São Teodoro de Nossa Senhora de Sion; **Gleides A. Nonato**, Colégio Amaldo; **Gustavo Henrique Pires**, Instituto Presbiteriano de Educação; **Marta Gabriella Brunale dos Reis**, Colégio Integrado Jaó; **Paula Conti dos Reis Santos**, Colégio Anglo-Latino; **Tânia M. Sasaki**, High Five Language Center.

South Korea **Don M. Ahn**, EDLS; **Don Bryant**, OnGok Middle School.

Taiwan **John A. Davey**, Stella Matutina Girls' High School, Taichung City, Taiwan; **Gregory Alan Gwenossis**, Victoria Academy.

Japan **Simon Butler**, Fujimi Junior and Senior High School; **Yuko Hiroyama**, Pioneer Language School; **Mark Itoh**, Honjo East Senior High School Affiliated Junior High School; **Norio Kawakubo**, Yokohama YMCA ACT; **Michael Lambe**, Kyoto Girls Junior and Senior High School; **John George Lowery**, Dokkyo Junior High School/John G. Lowery School of English; **Jacques Stearn**, American Language School; **Simon Wykamp**, Hiroshima Johoku Junior and Senior High School.

Illustration Credits

Ken Batelman 46, 49
Michael Brennan 115
David Coulson 30, 31, 42, 43, 52, 53, 60, 61, 80, 104
Bruce Day 11, 38, 39, 48, 70
James Elston 7, 20, 58, 118, 122, 123
Larry Jones 66, 72, 73, 87, 90
Frank Montagna 14, 15, 33, 37, 106, 107, 112, 113
Rob Schuster 32, 40, 77, 78, 114, 118, 119, 121
Jeff Shelley 4, 47, 57
James Yamasaki 28, 29
Sattu Rodrigues 36

Photo Acknowledgements

The authors and publishers acknowledge the following sources of copyright material and are grateful for the permissions granted. While every effort has been made, it has not always been possible to identify the sources of all the material used, or to trace all copyright holders. If any omissions are brought to our notice, we will be happy to include the appropriate acknowledgements on reprinting.

Student's Book

p. 6 (T): ©Westend61/Getty Images; p. 6 (TC): ©Comstock/Stockbyte/Getty Images; p.6 (BC): ©Nicholas Prior/The Image Bank/Getty Images; p.6 (B): ©Fuse/Getty Images; p.10: ©kali9/E+/Getty Images; p.12 (T): ©Colleen Cahill/Design Pics/Design Pics/Corbis; p.12 (C): ©Shmuel Thaler/Photolibrary/Getty Images; p.12 (B): © Adam Burn/Corbis; p.13: ©John Giustina/SuperStock/Corbis; p.16 (T): ©Izabela Habur/iStock/Getty Images Plus; p.18 (1): ©J Carter Rinaldi/FilmMagic/Getty Images; p.18 (2): ©Clive Brunskill/Getty Images; p.18 (3): ©COLUMBIA PICTURES / THE KOBAL COLLECTION; p.18 (4): ©Suhaimi Abdullah/Getty Images; p.18 (5): Christopher Polk/Getty Images for NARAS; p.18 (6): Han Myung-Gu/WireImage; p.18 (7): Mike Coppola/DCNYRE2015/Getty Images for dcp; p.19: ©Bruce Laurence/The Image Bank/Getty Images; p.20 (L): ©Bill Reitzel/Digital Vision/Getty Images; p.20 (C): © Blend Images/Alamy; p.20 (R): ©Sean De Burca/Corbis; p.21: ©Radius Images/Getty Images Plus; p.22 (TL): ©Jani Bryson/iStock / Getty Images Plus; p.22 (CL): ©arek_malang/Shutterstock; p.22 (BL): ©Denis Kuvaev/Shutterstock; p.22 (TR): ©Hill Street Studios/Nicole Goddard/Blend Images/Getty Images; p.22 (CR): ©Camille Tokerud/The Image Bank/Getty Images; p.22 (BR): ©RedChopsticks/Getty Images; p.23 (L): ©Jupiterimages/Stockbyte/Getty Images; p.23 (CL): ©Monkey Business Images/Shutterstock; p.23 (CR): ©Asia Images Group/Getty Images; p.23 (R): ©michaeljung/Shutterstock; p.24 (BR): ©Barbara Peacock/The Image Bank/Getty Images; p. 24: (tablet and smart phone): ©Youzitx/Getty Images; p.25 (BL): ©hadynyah/E+/Getty Images; p.25 (BCL): ©michaeljung/Shutterstock; p.25 (BCR): ©Vikram Raghuvanshi/

iStock / Getty Images Plus; p.25 (BR): ©Vincenzo Lombardo/Stockbyte/Getty Images; p. 25 (background): © roccomontoya/Getty Images; p.26 (TL): ©Chepe Nicoli/Shutterstock; p.26 (CL): Getty Images/Getty Images; p.26(BL): ©George Pimentel/WireImage/Getty Images; p.26 (TR): ©Warner Br/Everett/REX; p.26 (CR): ©Jeffrey Mayer/WireImage/Getty Images; p.26 (BR): ©George Doyle/Stockbyte/Getty Images; p.27: ©Reg Charity/Corbis; p.33 (B): The Asahi Shimbun/Getty Images; p.34 (a): ©CostinT/E+/Getty Images; p.34 (b): ©Valeri Potapova/Shutterstock; p.34 (c): ©GeorgeMPhotography/Shutterstock; p.34 (d): ©domnitsky/Shutterstock; p.34 (e): ©FERNANDO BLANCO CALZADA/Shutterstock; p.34 (f): ©berents/iStock/Getty Images Plus; p.35 (1): ©Michiel de Wit/Shutterstock; p.35 (2): ©Massimiliano Pieraccini/Shutterstock; p.35 (finger repeated 3 times): ©studioVin/Shutterstock; p.35 (3): ©i store/Alamy; p.35 (4): ©tankist276/Shutterstock; p.35 (hand): ƒVladislavGudovskiy/Shutterstock; p.35 (5): ©FERNANDO BLANCO CALZADA/Shutterstock; p.35 (6): ©nanD_Phanuwat/Shutterstock; p.36 (1): ©hamurishi/Shutterstock; p.36 (2): ©Mauricio de Sousa Editora Ltda; p.36 (3: bike): ©Ozger Aybike Sarikaya/Shutterstock; p.36 (3: character): ©Warner Br/Everett/REX; p.36 (4): ©Indigo Fish/Shutterstock; p.36 (5): ©Steven May/Alamy; p.36 (6 red): ©FlamingPumpkin/E+/Getty Images; p.36 (6 green): ©Michael Burrell/Alamy; p.40: ©Derek Latta/Photodisc/Getty; p.41: ©Ingram Publishing/Getty Images; p.43: ©Julia Ivantsova/Shutterstock; p.44 (a): ©Directphoto Collection/Alamy; p.44 (b): ©China Photos/Alamy; p.44 (c): ©IMAGEMORE Co.,Ltd./Getty Images; p.44 (d): © Kim Karpeles/Alamy; p.44 (e): ©Jeff Greenberg 2 of 6/Alamy; p.44 (f): ©Adisa/Shutterstock; p.50 (TL): ©David L. Moore/Alamy; p.50 (TR): ©VisitBritain/Doug McKinlay; p.50 (CL): © John James/Alamy; p.50 (CR): ©Tom Hopkins/Aurora/Getty Images; p.50 (BL): ©Rayman/Photographer's Choice RF/Getty Images; p.50 (BR): ©Kevin Britland/Alamy; p.54 (T): ©William Manning/Corbis; p.54 (B): ©Terrance Klassen/Alamy; p.55 (L): ©Sean Justice/The Image Bank/Getty Images; p.55 (R): ©Rob Lewine/Getty Images; p.62 (Jordan): ©Rob Lewine/Getty Images; p.62 (Lori): ©Digitalskillet/iStock / Getty Images Plus; p.62 (Chris): ©Johnny Greig/iStock / Getty Images Plus; p.62 (Jill): ©Samuel Borges Photography/Shutterstock; p.62 (Jerimiah): ©brbimages/E+/Getty Images; p.63 (BL): ©Tom Stewart/Corbis; p.63 (BC): ©StockLite/Shutterstock; p.63 (BR): ©Darama/Corbis; p.64 (1): ©Mitchell Funk/Photographer's Choice/Getty Images; p.64 (2): ©Susan Pease/Alamy; p.64 (3): ©Nancy Hoyt Belcher/Alamy; p.64 (4): Gavin Hellier/Robert Harding World Imagery/Getty Images; p.64 (5): ©Raymond Forbes/age fotostock/Getty Images; p.64 (6): ColorBlind Images/Iconica/Getty Images; p.67 (1): ©romakoma/Shutterstock; p.67 (2): © Mick Roessler/Corbis; p.67 (3): ©Pung/Shutterstock; p.68: ©RonTech200/E+/Getty Images; p.69: © Photo Network/Alamy; p.71: ©George Doyle/Stockbyte/Getty Imafes; p.74 (1): © Kinn Deacon/Alamy; p.74 (2): ©Aerial Archives/Alamy; p.74 (3): ©Steve Collender/Shutterstock; p.74 (4): ©LI CHAOSHU/Shutterstock; p.74 (5): ©Dale May/Corbis; p.74 (6): ©Comstock Images/Stockbyte/Getty Images; p.74 (7): ©Javier Larrea/age fotostock/Getty Images; p.74 (8): ©Jetta Productions/Digital Vision/Getty Images; p.74 (9): ©Baerbel Schmidt/Stone/Getty Images; p.76 (TL): ©nevodka/Shutterstock; p.76 (TR): ©Jamie Grill/Iconica/Getty Images; p.76 (CR): ©Hurst Photo/Shutterstock ; p.76 (BL): ©Tomasz Trojanowski/Shutterstock ; p.76 (BR): ©photogl/Shutterstock; p.82 (T): © Hero Images Inc./Hero Images Inc./Corbis; p.82 (C): © Hero Images/Corbis; p.82 (B): ©Larry Dle Gordon/The Image Bank/Getty Images; p.83: ©Goodshot/Getty Images Plus/Getty Images; p.84 (T): ©SNEHIT/Shutterstock; p.84 (B): Dennis O'Clair/The Image Bank/Getty Images; p.85 (TL): ©dwphotos/Shutterstock; p.85 (TR): ©Umberto Shtanzman/Shutterstock; p.85 (BL): ©Maria Dryfhout/Shutterstock; p.85 (BR): ©Zadorozhnyi Viktor/Shutterstock; p.88 (TL): ©Lawrence Lucier/FilmMagic/Getty Images; p.88 (TR): ©Jason Miller/Getty Images; p.88 (BL): ©Steve Babineau/NBAE via Getty Images; p.88 (BR): ©Dave J Hogan/Getty Images; p.89 (T): ©Mireya Acierto/Getty Images; p.89 (B): ©GONZALO/Bauer-Griffin/GC Images; p.92 (1): ©Andrew Olney/Digital Vision/Getty Images; p.92 (2): ©Zadorozhnyi Viktor/Shutterstock; p.92 (3): ©Jose Luis Pelaez Inc/Blend Images/Getty Images; p.92 (4): © Ingram Publishing/Alamy; p.92 (5): ©Richard Levine/Alamy; p.92 (6): © Pontino/Alamy; p.93 (T): © F1online digitale Bildagentur GmbH / Alamy; p.93 (B): ©Richard Levine/Alamy; p.95 (TL): ©Rob Lewine/Getty Images; p.95 (TR): ©Radius Images/Getty Images; p.95 (BR): ©Romiana Lee/Shutterstock; p.96: ©Timothy A. Clary/AFP/Getty Images; p.97: ©B2M Productions/Photographer's Choice RF/Getty Images; p.98 (L): ©Koichi Kamoshida/Getty Images; p.98 (TC): Frazer Harrison/Getty Images for 102.7 KIIS FM's Wango Tango; p.98 (TR): Clemens Bilan/Getty Images; p.98 (BL): Jemal Countess/Getty Images; p.98 (BR):©Jamie McCarthy/WireImage; p.100 (L): ©Tyler Boyes/Shutterstock; p.100 (C): ©npine/Shutterstock; p.100 (R): © Rodolfo Arpia/Alamy; p.101 (T): © F1online digitale Bildagentur GmbH / Alamy; p.101 (C): JTB/UIG via Getty Images; p.101 (B): ©Image Source/Getty Images; p.102 (TL): ©Sean Justice/The Image Bank/Getty Images; p.102 (TC): ©Steven May/Alamy; p.102 (TR): ©Andersen Ross/Stockbyte/Getty Images; p.102 (BL): ©Ned Frisk/Corbis; p.102 (BC): ©James Darell/Digital Vision/Getty Images; p.102 (BR): ©Windzepher/iStock/Getty Images Plus; p. 105 (TL): ©David R. Frazier Photolibrary, Inc./Alamy; p. 105 (TC): ©Peter Gridley/Stockbyte/Getty Images; p. 105 (TR): ©Fraser Hall/Photographer's Choice RF/Getty Images; p. 105 (BL): ©Chad Slattery/The Image Bank/Getty Images; p. 105 (BC): ©ShootingCompany/Alamy; p. 105(BR): ©Fuse/Getty Images; p.108 (1): ©Jose Luis Pelaez Inc/Blend Images/Getty Images; p.108 (2): ©LWA/Dann Tardif/Blend Images/Getty Images; p.108 (3): ©Corbis; p.108 (4): ©altrendo images/Getty Images; p.108 (5): ©Ant Strack/Corbis; p.108 (6): ©JeffreyIsaacGreenberg/Alamy; p.108 (7): ©Andersen Ross/The Image Bank/Getty Images; p.108 (8): ©Jennifer Boggs/Photolibrary/Getty Images; p.110: ©Richard Levine/Alamy; p.111: ©Image Source/Getty Images; p.116 (1): ©Aaron Amat/Shutterstock; p.116 (2): ©SAIndor Kelemen/iStock / Getty Images Plus; p.116 (3): ©Gyvafoto/Shutterstock; p.116 (4): ©Oleksiy Mark/iStock / Getty Images Plus; p.116 (5): ©Siede Preis/Photodisc/Getty Images; p.116 (6): ©Theerapol Pongkangsananan/Shutterstock; p.116 (7): ©Everything/Shutterstock; p.116 (8): ©Chiyacat/Shutterstock; p.116 (9): ©Gayvoronskaya_Yana/Shutterstock; p.116 (10): ©MarkHededus/iStock / Getty Images Plus; p.116 (11): ©Konjushenko Vladimir/Shutterstock; p.116 (12): ©Robnroll/Shutterstock; p.120 (1): Corbis; p.120 (2): ©Jorg Hackemann/Shutterstock; p.120 (3): ©Leslie Richard Jacobs/Corbis; p.120 (4): ©Dafinka/Shutterstock; p.120 (5): ©Justin Atkins/Shutterstock; p.120 (6): isitsharp/Vetta/Getty Images; p.120 (7): ©Owen Franken/CORBIS; p.120 (8): ©Otto Rogge/CORBIS; p.125: ©dbimages/Alamy; p.126 (T): ©Rick Gomez/Blend Images/Corbis; p.126 (BL): ©Bloomimage/Corbis; p.126 (BCL): ©Comstock/Stockbyte/Getty Images; p.126 (BCR): ©jaroon/iStock/Getty Images Plus; p.126 (BR): ©Samuel Borges Photography/Shutterstock; p.127 (T): ©Stockbyte/Getty Images; p.127 (C): ©Juanmonino/iStock/Getty Images Plus/Getty Images; p.127 (B): ©Mark Bowden/E+/Getty Images; p.128 (TR): ©LdF/E+/Getty Images; p.128 (TC): ©Oleksiy Mark/iStock / Getty Images Plus; p.128 (TL): ©SA!ndor Kelemen/iStock / Getty Images Plus; p.128 (TV): ©Piotr Adamowicz/Shutterstock; p.128 (game): ©forest_strider/iStock / Getty Images Plus; p.128 (MP3): ©trucic/Shutterstock; P.128 (clock): ©Crisp/Shutterstock; p.128 (computer): ©scanrail/iStock / Getty Images Plus; p.129 (TL): © Mathias Beinling / Alamy; p.129 (TR): © Kim Karpeles / Alamy; p.129 (C): © Emily Riddell/Alamy; p.129 (B): © Robert Harding World Imagery / Alamy; p.130 (T): © Rob Lewine/Tetra Images/Corbis; p.130 (B): ©Daniel M Ernst/Shutterstock; p.131 (TL): ©charistoone-travel/Alamy; p.131 (TR): © Jim West/Alamy; p.131 (media centre): © dpa picture alliance / Alamy; p.131 (football): © PCN Photography / Alamy; p.131 (swim): ©withGod/Shutterstock; p.132 (T): ©Johnny Greig/Alamy; p.132 (CL): ©SeanPavonePhoto/iStock / Getty Images Plus; p.132 (CR): ©John W Banagan/Photographer's Choice/Getty Images; p.132 (B): © Kim Kyung-Hoon/Reuters/Corbis; p. 133 (TL): ©Preto Perola/Shutterstock; p.133 (TR): ©hamurishi/Shutterstock

Commissioned photography by Lawrence Migdale for pages 2, 3, 5 (T & B), 8 (TL, TR, BL & BR), 9, 16 (TL, TR, BL, CR & BR), 17, 24 (L, TC, TR & BC), 25 (TL, TCL, TCR & TR), 33 (T), 36 (TL, BR); 45 (L & R), 51, 63 (T), 64 (7 & 8), 75, 79, 81, 91, 94, 103, 109 (L & R).

Cover photograph by Joe McBride/Getty Images.

Art Direction, book design, and layout services: A+ Comunicação, São Paulo